DATE DUE

GAYLORD			PRINTED IN U.S.A.

MOVIE MAKING COURSE

PRINCIPLES, PRACTICE, AND TECHNIQUES:
THE ULTIMATE GUIDE FOR THE ASPIRING FILMMAKER

CHRIS PATMORE

BARRON'S

A QUARTO BOOK

First edition for the United States,
Canada, and its territories and
possessions by Barron's Educational
Series, Inc. 2005.

All inquiries should be addressed to:
Barron's Educational Series, Inc.
250 Wireless Boulevard
Hauppauge, NY 11788
www.barronseduc.com

ISBN-13: 978-0-7641-3191-2

ISBN-10: 0-7641-3191-5

Library of Congress Catalog Card No.:
2004111722

QUAR.CSF

Conceived, designed, and produced by
Quarto Publishing plc
The Old Brewery
6 Blundell Street
London N7 9BH

Project editor Jo Fisher
Art editor Anna Knight
Designer James Lawrence
Illustrators Mark Duffin, Kuo Kang Chen
Assistant art director Penny Cobb
Photographer Paul Forrester
Copy editor Tom Neville
Art director Moira Clinch
Publisher Paul Carslake

Manufactured by Provision (Pte) Ltd,
Singapore
Printed by SNP Leefung Printers Ltd,
China

9 8 7 6 5 4 3 2 1

CONTENTS

INTRODUCTION

SO YOU WANT TO BE A FILMMAKER. YOU HAVE DREAMS OF WORKING WITH MEGABUCK HOLLYWOOD BUDGETS, MIXING WITH THE GLITTERATI AS YOUR EPIC *OEUVRE* FILLS THE SILVER SCREEN BEFORE A RAPTUROUS AUDIENCE. MAYBE YOU'LL BE LUCKY AND YOUR DREAM WILL COME TRUE, BUT IF FAME AND FORTUNE ARE YOUR MOTIVATIONS FOR MAKING A MOVIE, YOU SHOULD PROBABLY BE LOOKING FOR ANOTHER CAREER.

LIKE ANY FORM OF ART (AND FILMMAKING IS ESSENTIALLY A CREATIVE PURSUIT, DESPITE SOME OF WHAT COMES OUT OF HOLLYWOOD), MAKING A MOVIE REQUIRES VISION AND PASSION, RATHER THAN AMBITION. IF YOU HAVE THESE QUALITIES, YOU ARE WELL ON THE WAY TO MAKING YOUR FIRST MOVIE. IT MAY NOT BE *Citizen Kane*, BUT IT WILL BE ALL YOUR OWN WORK.

DREAM ON ▶▶
Alfred Hitchcock and Paul Newman on the set of *Torn Curtain* (1966). Big budgets, big stars, and a big reputation are what most budding filmmakers dream of, but you have to start somewhere and short movies are the best place to start.

WHY SHORT FILMS?

This book isn't about how to make Hollywood blockbusters, or even feature films; it's about making short films. Short films provide an affordable way to learn your craft and hone your skills. Whatever you learn making short films will transfer to larger productions. In fact, telling a story in ten minutes can be a lot harder than telling one in 90 minutes. It's all about economy, but that doesn't mean budget.

NO MORE EXCUSES

The aim of this book is to give you a grounding in the technology and methodology of moviemaking with little or no money, commonly known as *lo-no budget*, or sometimes *guerrilla*, filmmaking. There are many books on this subject, and on every other aspect of filmmaking, as you will have noticed if you have browsed your local or online bookseller. This book has been designed to be as concise as possible because one of the greatest enemies of the novice filmmaker is procrastination. "I'll make my film when I've read this book or that book"; "I can't do it until I have enough money for a crew and equipment." The excuses go on and on. This short book is filled with the information you need to start making a movie with almost no money, so you can forget about them. Although attending film school may be exciting and intellectually stimulating, experience is still going to be your best teacher.

The advice always given to budding authors is "Read a lot and write a lot." The same goes for aspiring filmmakers. Watch lots of movies on DVD (with the commentaries on)—you have a film school right there, with the best visiting lecturers possible. And with all the money you save from not having to pay for classes, you can go out and shoot lots of your own movies. In fact, the less money you have with which to make your films, the more inventive you will have to be. You can't lose. Even if you never earn any money from your movies, making them is still a relatively cheap, fun, and satisfying pastime.

After all the technical information, the Projects chapter has some ideas to help you get started, just in case you need a little inspiration. They cover a variety of genres, so there should be something there to get you motivated. So start making movies, and who knows if your dreams will come true? They don't call Hollywood the dream factory for nothing.

HISTORY

MOST PEOPLE START MAKING SHORT FILMS BECAUSE THEY HAVE NEITHER ACCESS TO GOOD EQUIPMENT NOR ANY EXPERIENCE, AND THAT IS ALSO HOW IT WAS IN THE EARLY DAYS OF CINEMA. THE VERY FIRST FILMS WERE NOTHING MORE THAN TECHNICAL EXPERIMENTS MADE BY INVENTORS. THE LUMIÈRE BROTHERS SIMPLY FILMED SOMETHING CLOSE AT HAND (WORKERS LEAVING THE FAMILY'S FACTORY) WHEN TRYING OUT THEIR INVENTION, THE CINÉMATOGRAPHE, JUST AS YOU WOULD WHEN YOU BUY A NEW CAMERA.

The earliest films were nearly all of a documentary nature. There was a particular fascination with trains and other forms of transportation, probably because the films were being made by scientists and engineers, but once cameras were in the hands of artists a whole new world of possibilities opened up.

After the initial excitement and novelty of seeing trains arriving in stations or racing along tracks, the public wanted something more entertaining. Even in cinema's infancy, filmmakers were experimenting with special effects, many of which were discovered by accident, often through using faulty equipment. One such accident (a camera jammed for a while; the resulting film recorded people magically appearing from nowhere and disappearing, while a carriage appeared to transmute into a hearse) inspired French magician and filmmaker Georges Méliès to make his first fantasy film. He went on to make more than 500 short films, with undoubtedly his most famous, A Trip to the Moon (1902), combining live action and simple animation.

The early pioneers also developed techniques, such as extreme close-ups, dolly shots, and even intercut edits, that remain staples of modern cinema. It was these innovations that finally set the stage and cinema apart as ways of telling stories, as well as film's lack of sound, of course.

PUBLIC DEMAND

As acceptance of the medium grew, so did its popularity. Filmmakers such as D. W. Griffiths started to produce longer and longer narrative movies, and the public was willing to pay a premium to see them. For practical reasons, animations, newsreels, and even comedies were not adapted to longer running times, so the short film came into its own.

In the early 1920s the films of Charlie Chaplin, W. C. Fields, and Laurel and Hardy, and animations by Max Fleischer and

A TRIP TO THE MOON ⬆
The most famous work from prolific short filmmaker, Georges Méliès, mixed live action with animation.

the newcomer, Walt Disney, proved very popular and often attracted bigger audiences than the features they accompanied. Their popularity made them perfect vehicles for experimentation with the latest development—synchronized sound.

ARRIVAL OF THE SHORT FILM

Unfortunately, this great advance in cinema entertainment coincided with the Great Depression, when going to the movies was not the first thing on most people's minds. In order to attract audiences, the Hollywood studios put a lot of effort into making quality, entertaining shorts, establishing departments dedicated to producing a constant flow of comedies and cartoons.

But not all shorts were slapstick. Many dramas were also produced, as were the cliffhanger serials that later inspired the Indiana Jones films. However, despite their popularity, short films were still considered the poor cousins of the feature-length B-movies and were therefore given third-rate facilities. It was television that eventually killed the Hollywood cinema shorts industry, but the new medium also provided work for a whole new generation of short-filmmakers, with an ever-increasing number of half-hour slots that needed filling. Animators found their work in demand, filling those 30-minute slots with 10-minute cartoons such as the ever-popular *Looney Tunes*. The arrival of commercial television also saw the development of a whole new type of short film—the advertisement—that has remained one of the most influential kinds shown.

Throughout this period, European filmmakers were producing less commercial, more experimental short films. They were more interested in creating art than entertainment, whether it was live action or animation, and much of this work permeated the feature films that subsequently influenced filmmakers internationally.

CHARLIE CHAPLIN ◀◀
His short silent films, in which he played the Little Tramp, made him an international household name and they are still popular today.

LAUREL AND HARDY ▲
This comic duo successfully made the transition to talkies by maintaining the short format for ever-popular, one-gag movies.

Although the popularity of short films waned during the 1970s as independent filmmakers concentrated on features, relegating the form to the ranks of amateurs and artists, it is now very much back in vogue, thanks mostly to affordable digital-video cameras and editing systems. More and more people are taking the chance to make short films and get them seen, both over the Internet and at the ever-increasing number of film festivals. While the quality is not always great (who said feature films are always well made?), real talent usually shines through.

As for the future, as long as people make movies there will always be someone making shorts and someone willing to watch them. It will not be how we make them but how we watch them that will change.

15 MINUTES OF FAME

THIS IS THE STORY OF ONE FILMMAKER'S EFFORTS TO TELL A SIMPLE AND PROFOUND STORY ON A RELATIVELY LOW BUDGET, AND ITS SUBSEQUENT INTERNATIONAL SUCCESS. IT SHOWS WHAT IS POSSIBLE TO ACHIEVE WITH A WELL-MADE SHORT FILM, AND IS HERE TO INSPIRE YOU.

THE YOUNG STAR ▲
A shot from the film, in which Jamal, the "terrorist," hides from the border guards pursuing him.

Ashvin Kumar is one of the new generation of filmmakers (another is Asif Kapadia, who directed *The Warrior*, 2001) who are trying to show that there is more to Indian films than Bollywood, and to create majestic narrative films in the tradition of Satyajit Ray.

After studying media and communication, Ashvin started making video shorts, commercials, and music videos in London, as well as setting up a digital post-production business in New Delhi, India. After briefly attending film school, he decided the money would be better spent on making a film on his own and using that as his education. The resulting 48-minute featurette, *Road to Ladakh* (2003), received a positive reaction and was shown internationally. It was too long to be entered into short-film competitions, so Ashvin wrote a 15-minute film based around the true story of a 12-year-old Pakistani boy who accidentally crossed the border into India.

Production of *Little Terrorist* began in November 2003. With a budget of only around $27,000 to complete a 15-minute 35mm film, Ashvin placed an ad on shootingpeople.org, the filmmakers' international networking Web site, and found a crew willing both to work for nothing and to pay their own travel expenses to India.

Apart from answering the need for genuine settings and native actors, shooting in India meant that production costs could be kept to a minimum. However, working in India comes with its own complications. Shooting in the Rajasthani desert meant extremes of temperature, even in January, the coolest part of the year. The intense contrast of the sunlight presented extra problems for the director of photography (DoP), as did the speed with which the light dropped at sunset.

DIRECTOR AT WORK ▲
Director, Ashvin Kumar (at right), and DoP, Markus Huersch, discuss the best way to shoot a scene.

LITTLE TERRORIST ▲
A publicity poster for the film, which was eventually nominated for an Academy Award.

DISASTER STRIKES ▲
At one point, fire destroyed the tent containing all the production's film stock. The film survived.

ACCOMMODATING THE EQUIPMENT ◀◀
The house where the main action takes place had to be specially built to allow easy access for the camera, lights, and grips.

AN UNEXPECTED AUDIENCE ◀◀
Crowds of curious onlookers put the production, and their own lives, at risk as they watched from the edge of the quarry.

With just six days scheduled for the shoot, there was very little room for errors or the unexpected (such as the tent containing the film burning down—the film was saved—and 200 villagers from the surrounding area arriving to watch, making sound-recording a nightmare). Working almost entirely with inexperienced, non-English-speaking actors and local crew meant communication was often slow. In spite of these minor obstacles, the shoot wrapped on schedule, avoiding excess charges on the camera that the budget could not support.

With the film in the can, writer/director/producer Ashvin put on his editor's cap to bring his vision to completion. The original score, composed by Nainita Desai, was interwoven with Indian folk music recorded on location, performed by the Ianngar troupe, who also appeared in the film as wandering minstrels.

The finished film had its world premiere at the Montreal World Film Festival in September 2004, where it won first prize. By the end of 2004 it had been accepted for 20 film festivals, winning first prizes in two of them and collecting a nomination for the European Academy Awards. At the Manhattan Shorts Film Festival the film won the Audience Award. The prize was sponsorship of equipment and services for making the winner's first feature film, including a camera for two months, lighting and grip package, $50,000 worth of vouchers for lab work and sound-mixing, and eight weeks of post-production and

THE MAIN SET ▲
The exterior of the main location set, a village house.

BUILDING TOWERS ▲
The sets were built using local know-how and labor.

editing—invaluable for the low-budget filmmaker. The flurry of recognition culminated in *Little Terrorist*'s nomination for the Best Short Film Oscar at the 2005 Academy Awards.

In 18 months the film had gone from a concept in London to the deserts of Rajasthan to the glamor of Hollywood's most prestigious event, thanks to the filmmaker's clarity of vision and determination, and the support of the film community at a very grassroots level. Stories like Ashvin's (and of others such as Asif Kapadia and Robert Rodriguez) show what commitment and talent can achieve.

VIDEO CAMERAS

IF YOU WANT TO MAKE A MOVIE, YOU WILL NEED A CAMERA (UNLESS YOUR INTENTION IS TO DO ANIMATION). MOVIE CAMERAS GIVE YOU A CHOICE OF TWO MEDIA—FILM OR VIDEOTAPE—AND WITHIN THOSE CATEGORIES YOU HAVE A CHOICE OF FORMATS. DIGITAL VIDEO (DV) IS ALL THE RAGE AT THE MOMENT AND IS LARGELY RESPONSIBLE FOR THE RESURGENCE OF THE SHORT FILM.

▶▶ Digital: The advantages

▶▶ Value for money

CAMERA PARTS ⯯

All video cameras are made of the same basic components, but each model has its own individual style and features, such as this HDR-FX1, Sony's first consumer level HDV (High Definition Video) model.

Microphone: Look for sockets for external mics—these will give you a more controllable sound recording. XLR inputs are best but are found only on top range cameras.

Lens hoods: Stop extraneous light from entering the lens and causing "flaring" bright beams of light that mar the image.

Hot shoe: For attaching accessories such as extra microphones or lights.

Viewing monitor: Adjustable screen that allows easy viewing from any angle or camera position. Generally not accurate enough for reliable color balance or exposure.

Viewfinder: Contains a tiny digital screen. Not as accurate as the optical finder on a film camera.

Battery: Removable batteries are crucial when shooting away from the power source.

Tape: Easy access to the tape is important for quick changing of media.

Manual override buttons: These give more control of the camera's functions.

Zoom lens: Most cameras have fixed lenses, except the Canon XL and expensive professional models. Look at the optical zoom range (usually around 10x).

3 CCD: The number of image capture chips. 3 CCD are best, although some single CCD cameras can produce excellent results.

Focus ring: An easy-to-access manual focus will give your videos a more professional look.

Iris control: Found on more expensive cameras, it adjusts the amount of light going through the lens.

There are many different DV formats available, from the consumer miniDV up to the professional High Definition Video (HDV) that has been used for films such as the Star Wars series.

WHICH FORMAT?

For our purposes miniDV is most likely to be the first choice, although DVCAM, Digital Betacam (DigiBeta), and the new range of HDV cameras are viable, if more costly, alternatives. It is best to stick with digital video rather than some of the older analog formats such as VHS, S-VHS, Hi-8, or even professional Beta because, apart from the low resolution of the consumer formats, there is the additional expense and inconvenience of digitizing footage to take advantage of computer editing. Another advantage of the digital format is its ability to maintain the quality of the original no matter how many times it is copied.

Although miniDV has been used for major theatrical releases, including *The Blair Witch Project* (Eduardo Sánchez and Daniel Myrick), *Time Code* (Mike Figgis), *Full Frontal* (Steven Soderbergh), and *28 Days Later* (Danny Boyle), it has been chosen in order to exploit the fact that the movie is obviously not shot on film. If your intention is merely to learn the craft of moviemaking and possibly to enter competitions or festivals, make DVDs, show on your local cable station, or broadcast over the Internet, then the DV format is perfect.

BUYING ADVICE

If you are buying your first DV camera, try to avoid cheaper models. Their lack of important features—a

PRO-LEVEL CAMERA ▶▶
Sony is always at the forefront of consumer-priced pro-level cameras. Its PDX10 offers DVCAM, 3 CCD, and XLR inputs at a price lower than similar cameras cost at used prices.

HIGH-DEFINITION VIDEO CAMERA ▲
JVC produced one of the first "consumer" High Definition (HD) cameras, offering broadcast quality at an affordable price. Other manufacturers soon followed up with their own range of cameras. The features and price competition can only benefit filmmakers.

ADAPTABLE & VERSATILE ▶▶
Canon's XL DV camera is popular with a huge range of filmmakers, both in Hollywood (Steven Soderbergh, Danny Boyle) and among independents. Besides cool looks, one of its biggest advantages is interchangeable lenses. The XL2 (pictured) also has progressive scan and true 16:9 widescreen.

RENT OR BUY?

The format you choose will depend on your budget and the intended purpose of the finished movie. If you know you are going to be broadcast, DVCAM or DigiBeta are your best solutions, as they will provide high-resolution and shoot true 16:9 aspect. They are expensive, but not prohibitively so, providing you are going to get commercial use from them.

For a one-time or occasional shoot, by all means rent. Because technology advances so fast these days, renting will ensure that you either get the very latest kit, or older cameras at a reduced rate.

With consumer and "prosumer" cameras, the retail market is so competitive that you can get finance deals with delayed payments that could allow you to start earning before you have to part with any cash, making rental unnecessary. In the end it's all about balancing the budget and making the best-quality viewable movie you can.

quality lens, decent resolution, external microphone jack, and DV in/DV out—may hinder your work. As technology and manufacturing improve, the quality-to-price ratio moves in favor of the buyer. Use the many consumer magazines available to ascertain which models offer the best value for the money.

Judicious use of money is one of the secrets of low-budget filmmaking, in contrast to Hollywood's approach to solving problems by throwing dollars at them. When buying a camera, don't spend more than you need to, but don't try to save money at the expense of useful features. On the other hand, don't use the lack of camera features as an excuse for not shooting a movie. Even the lowest-spec DV camera will have more features than some of the older pro models.

In fact, there is quite a lot to be said for using a simple camera, as it will make you concentrate on telling your story rather than being hung up on the technology. On the other hand, poor quality pictures and sound are not going to impress an audience.

The big advantage of DV is the cost of the media. In fact, the discounted retail cost for two hours of 16mm film with processing and telecine (not including camera costs) is about the same as buying a semi-pro DV camera and 12 hours of tape. The downside of originating digitally becomes apparent if you want to show your movie in theaters, because transferring from tape to 35mm is very expensive. If your DV film is picked up for movie theater distribution, however, you can get the distributor to pay for the conversion.

FILM CAMERAS

The whole art form and its surrounding industry take their names from this medium. Within the category of film you have a choice of formats. Deciding which medium and format to go with will be dictated by what you intend to do with your finished movie and by your budget. Generally, these two factors are inseparable.

BOLEX RX5 ▲

The venerable Bolex 16mm cameras have been the workhorses of independent filmmakers for decades and come in clockwork (really!) and battery-powered versions. Used ones can be found at reasonable prices.

» 16mm: Best choice for low-budget moviemaking

» Standard vs Super16

» Smaller format: Super 8

FILM

Money is always going to be the deciding factor when choosing a format. Within the scope of this book, 35mm film does not really enter into consideration. It is a professional format that requires serious money. Even using all the cunning methods that "guerrilla" filmmakers have developed for getting something for nothing, you would be very lucky to be able to shoot your first film on this format. If you have the means to make a 35mm film, this book probably isn't for you anyway.

Down from 35mm is 16mm. This is the ideal format for shooting independent, low-budget celluloid-based movies. The film stock is cheaper than 35mm, as are the cameras. Quality is high and the movie can be enlarged to 35mm if you somehow end up getting a theatrical release. Nearly all the breakout independent filmmakers used this format for their first features—Kevin Smith (*Clerks*), Robert Rodriguez

(*El Mariachi*), Spike Lee (*She's Gotta Have It*), Michael Moore (*Roger and Me*), to name a few. If you are serious about working the festivals circuit, 16mm has to be your choice, although digital video is gaining greater acceptance every year.

Within the 16mm format you have two choices: standard 16mm and Super 16. Standard 16mm used to be the favored format for television, as it uses the same 4:3 ratio, and it can easily be striped for sound. The advantage of Super 16 is its widescreen format of 1.66:1, which is very close to the 16:9 ratio of HDTV. It is also best suited to enlarging to 35mm for theatrical release. Unfortunately, the larger image area uses the edge of the film where the soundtrack would usually go. Super 16 requires a special camera, and the necessary projectors are not common.

SMALL FORMAT

Down from 16mm is Super 8. Before the arrival of the camcorder, this was the format favored for home movies. The film came in 50-foot cartridges (2 minutes 30 seconds at 24 frames per second) that

CLASSIC 16 ▶▶

For those who feel nervous about buying used equipment, pro8mm.com sells refurbished 16mm cameras at reasonable prices.

PROS:

Quality: Film gives better resolution and color.

Control: Easier to vary speed for slow motion.

Distribution: Most theaters are only geared for projecting film, although this is changing.

Archival: Film is less likely to suffer technological obsolescence.

CLASSIC SUPER 8 PRO CAMERA ▲ PRO8 FILM ◄◄

For shooting Super 8, pro8mm.com is probably one of your best resources, supplying a complete range of films, processing, and telecine services, and a range of new and refurbished cameras. eBay is a good source for used cameras. Braun Nizo, Canon, Beaulieu, and Nalcom are all excellent choices.

CONS:

Cost: Equipment and media are expensive. Film and processing costs don't allow for experimentation or mistakes.

Expertise: Good results require knowledge of celluloid, lighting, and exposure.

Crew: At least one additional person for sound will be needed.

were simply dropped into the camera for shooting and, when finished, sent to a lab for developing. The format is far too small to be really practical for anything serious, unless you want to get that home-movie look, or you want to shoot film and have a very low budget. There are still a couple of camera manufacturers but secondhand ones can be bought very cheaply from sources like eBay. As with all film, shooting on Super 8 can be quite expensive when compared to the latest digital video (DV) cameras, but it still has a dedicated following (see pages 116–117).

Shooting film isn't just a matter of getting hold of a camera, especially in the case of 16mm, as you also have to look at different lenses, a light meter, and sound-recording equipment. Unlike video, you cannot record sound directly into the camera, so you will definitely need a suitable tape recorder. Although the Nagra reel-to-reel was the standard for decades, DAT (Digital Audio Tape) has captured the market because of its quality, convenience, and price. More about sound on pages 72–75.

To complete your basic kit list you are going to need camera supports and editing equipment. These are covered on pages 16–17 and 86–91.

RENT OR BUY?

35mm film will be beyond most budgets and would be a rental job no matter what. When it comes to 16mm, the decision to rent or buy will depend on the seriousness of your project and your commitment to making further films. If it is a professional job and you have no other access to a camera (friends, college), then rental is your only option. You will get modern, reliable equipment that is regularly serviced and, if it should break down in the middle of shooting, you can be fairly sure of getting some sort of replacement. The rental is also a legitimate expense that can be written off. Rental makes even more sense for funded feature films.

Sometimes you may be lucky enough to find or be offered a camera at a very low price. Make sure it is reliable and will do what you want it to. The disadvantage of buying is that if the camera breaks down you are left with the repair and service bills and no way to finish your shoot. If you are just making shorts for yourself as a learning experience, with very few other people involved, then one of these bargain cameras may serve you well, and will get the job done, providing you can work within its limitations. And you can usually sell the camera later, without huge financial loss.

EXTRA GEAR

ONCE YOU HAVE CHOSEN YOUR CAMERA FORMAT, WHETHER VIDEO OR FILM, YOU WILL STILL NEED SOME ANCILLARY EQUIPMENT TO SUPPORT IT— LITERALLY. A HOST OF DEVICES ARE AVAILABLE TO HELP YOU STABILIZE YOUR CAMERA, FROM TRIPODS TO DOLLIES AND CRANES, TO A VARIETY OF STEADICAM-TYPE UNITS. ALL COME WITH A PURPOSE AND A PRICE TAG.

- ▸▸ Camera supports
- ▸▸ Clapperboard
- ▸▸ Computer

SUPPORT

The most useful provider of support has to be the tripod (legs). When it comes to video tripods, it is wise to spend a little bit more than you can really afford, and go for the best. Many professional units are sold in two parts, legs and head, with the head being the more important and expensive. When shooting movies you must have a fluid head. A normal camera tripod is adequate if you are using it just for static (locked-down) shots, but when it comes to movements such as panning (following action horizontally) or tilting (vertical movement), it is not smooth enough, and your camerawork will be jerky, but without the rawness of being handheld.

Apart from the quality of movements possible with the more expensive fluid-head tripods, they usually come with options that make them easily adaptable to other supports, such as jibs and dollies. These will increase the professional look of your camera movements.

There are cheaper, consumer-level, fluid-head tripods that are serviceable, but if you are serious about making movies, then invest in a quality stand from a company such as Miller. It will last for years and won't suffer from obsolescence the way other

FLOWPOD ▸▸
To smooth out the jolting of handheld camera work, especially while walking or running, some sort of stabilizer is needed. Full Steadicam rigs cost thousands and usually require an experienced operator. Economical alternatives, such as the FlowPod, will do a serviceable job, although they will never match a body-worn stabilizer.

FLUID HEAD ▾
Fluid head tripods are essential for smooth movement when filming, which is even more important when using video. Get one to match your camera—not too heavy or too light. Make sure it is adjustable to a variety of heights and can also be adapted for use with dollies and jibs. This model is produced by Miller, which holds the first patent for fluid heads and makes a range of tripods and heads.

LIGHTWEIGHT TRIPOD COMPACTED ▴
Ranging from 63 in. (see photo at right) to a compact 27 in. (see above), this adjustable tripod can handle a camcorder up to 20 lbs.

LIGHTWEIGHT TRIPOD ◂◂
This tripod combines a 75mm fluid pan-and-tilt ball head with a light, solid, spreaderless tripod. Features include a selectable counter-balance, bubble level, and a 5.5 lb. weight.

technology does. The fact that a tripod is almost impossible to find secondhand really shows how valuable it is—and should you need to sell it, it won't lose its value.

The other type of support is a rig worn by an operator, which allows him to move around and follow the action. It incorporates mechanisms that absorb the jiggling movement of walking to give a smooth flow. These rigs are very expensive, but there are some cheaper alternatives designed for DV cameras, which also double as monopods.

Other hardware you may need includes lights (see pages 52–55) and sound-recording equipment (see pages 72–75), depending on your shoot and camera. Apart from these, there are many bits and pieces to take with you on the shoot, not least of which is the clapperboard, or slate.

MAKING A CLEAN SLATE

Your shoot won't seem like a real movie without a clapperboard. Buying one from a specialist will cost a lot. Suppliers usually offer a choice of the traditional blackboard type or the contemporary white dryboard. There are also digital versions that mark timecode, but they are extremely expensive and are not necessary. Blackboard clappers can be found in gift and gadget shops at a fraction of what you will pay in a pro shop, and will work just as well.

You only need to use a clapperboard if you are recording sound separately from the pictures, as the "clack" acts as a visual and auditory marker for synching. If you are shooting synched sound on video you can use a slate, which is simply a board onto which you write all the relevant information before each take. You can easily make your own at a minimal cost with a small, dry-wipe memo board that you can divide into the relevant sections with an indelible pen. It serves as a marker and, when used with the shooting list, makes editing much easier, especially if your camera shows timecode.

HARDWARE ▶▶
Apple's iMac offers lots of computing power in a compact design and comes with all the software you need to edit, add music to, and create DVDs of your films. It will also run Final Cut Pro (or Express), which is quickly becoming the standard for digital editing.

CLAPPERBOARD ▲
Clapperboards look great and add a touch of authenticity, but they are expensive and are really only necessary if shooting sound and images separately.

DIY SLATE ▲
When using video, you can make your own slate from a small, dry-wipe board. Draw it up, as shown, with an indelible marker pen, and use a dry-wipe pen to write up each take.

COMPUTER
The final piece of equipment you will need is some sort of computer for a range of tasks, from budgeting to script writing to editing. As with cameras, get the best you can afford, with the knowledge that it will be superseded with a cheaper and better model just after you've bought it. Any model from the Apple Macintosh range is an excellent choice, as their Final Cut editing software has established itself as the industry leader. Apple's eMac, iMac, and iBook ranges come equipped with all the software you need to produce a movie, even including making your own DVDs. (More on editing software on pages 86–91.)

READY TO SHOOT?
A camera, microphone, tripod (or some other sort of support), and computer are all the gear you need to start making your first short film—and some stock (film or tape), of course. There are dozens of accessories you can add to these basics, and they will be mentioned later. The important thing is to get started and familiarize yourself with your equipment.

BEFORE
YOU START

Filmmaking is both a solitary and a collective activity. The initial stage of writing the script is invariably done alone, pre-production with one or two trusted and responsible assistants, then the shoot with a cast and crew of however many it takes, finally finishing alone again for the editing. As the director, you can be isolated by your responsibilities, and it is how you deal with the weight of those responsibilities that will make the task enjoyable—or not.

One of the advantages of making a short film is that you get to taste a pared-down version of the production cycle. You carry out all the roles involved in making a feature film but in bite-size portions.

THREE STAGES

The three distinct stages of making a movie (pre-production, the shoot, post-production) are covered separately, and each of these sections is further divided into specific tasks. How many of these you carry out, and to what extent, will be up to you and the nature of your film, but the sooner you get into the habit of working systematically, the easier it will be to manage your burgeoning film career.

Pre-production is the foundation on which your film is built. There is an old saying that if you are doing a day's wood chopping you should spend the first seven hours sharpening the axe. Over the coming pages, the steps you need to take before shooting will be covered in more or less the order in which they need to be tackled. Let's get started.

DEVELOPING IDEAS

HUMAN NATURE IS RULED BY TWO BASIC PRINCIPLES: DESIRE AND ACTION. YOU GET AN IDEA AND YOU PUT IT INTO ACTION —OR AT LEAST THAT'S THE THEORY. AT THE MOST BASIC LEVEL, YOU NEED TO EAT, SO THE DESIRE TO EAT MOTIVATES YOU INTO SOME SORT OF ACTION TO FULFILL THAT WANT—LIKE STOPPING AT A FAST-FOOD RESTAURANT.

▸▸ Filming what you know: The documentary

▸▸ Stories: Making use of your limitations

KEEPING TABS ⬇
Read books and newspapers, watch television. Keep your finger on the pulse and take inspiration from what is going on around you.

The same happens with filmmaking, more or less. You get an idea for a story or documentary, you grab a camera and go and make it. Almost.

What usually happens is that you get an idea, and then spend the rest of the time finding reasons not to do it, most of which seem wholly justifiable. Or you have the camera and you're all fired up, but you haven't a clue what to shoot. To get started, the ideas person and the action person need to get together. After all, filmmaking is, by and large, a team pursuit, a meeting of individual talents and strengths.

FIRST IDEA

For the sake of this exercise, let's assume you don't have a network of filmmaking friends, but you do have a camera and want to start shooting your first film. Running around aiming the camera at anything that moves is a great way to familiarize yourself with its functions, and is a good thing to do before embarking on a serious project, but the result doesn't usually make great viewing. What you need is an idea.

This book is concerned with short films (movies, photoplays, or whatever you want to call them). One of the beauties of the format is that you can pick a single theme and explore it in as much depth as you think it merits in a minimal time. It can also be extremely challenging to convey an idea effectively in ten minutes.

If you are not an overly imaginative storyteller, then start with a documentary. New writers are often advised to write about what they know. Pick something you are passionate about, because if there is no passion being projected on the screen, you are

TAKE NOTE ▸▸
Don't let that brilliant idea you had on the bus disappear. Keep a notebook handy and get into the habit of writing down your ideas as you think of them.

going to lose your audience. It can be anything at all, from stamp collecting to your favorite local sports team. The more obscure the subject, the greater the need to approach it creatively. You will find more on making documentaries at the back of the book.

SHORT STORIES

If storytelling is your thing, the same rules apply— write about what you know and don't be too ambitious for your first efforts. Before you start writing, look around at what you have available to shoot with, in the way of actors, props, and locations.

Working within these limitations will help you to stretch your imagination and can have surprising results.

One of the biggest challenges is the time limit, and it is a good idea to set yourself a running time before you start. You don't have to be absolutely precise, but deciding on a "no-longer-than" and a "no-shorter-than" will make you more disciplined. Invariably, it is better to go for shorter than longer. It is amazing how much you can tell in five minutes, and how long 15 minutes can seem for a badly executed story.

As you start putting together your ideas, don't worry if they seem derivative. There isn't much that hasn't already been done; it will be up to your interpretation and vision to create something unique. The important thing is to get started, learn as you go, and above all be ruthlessly self-critical.

SEE ALSO

Pages 22–25 *Effective Storytelling*
Pages 106–109 *10-minute Documentary*

COLLECTING INSPIRATION ⌄

Once you have that all-important first idea, start collecting things related to that idea to inspire you. Postcards, for instance, and curios found at flea markets are always helpful. Keep track of your valuable finds in a journal.

UNLIKELY PREMISES FOR FILMS

Some of the most successful films ever made have been based on ideas that studio heads dismissed as not being marketable, but which came to fruition because of the tenacity of their directors. Here are ten such films. This is by no means a definitive list.

1   *Being John Malkovich:* An unsuccessful puppeteer discovers a portal that takes him into the brain of actor John Malkovich, and he tries to exploit the situation.

2   *Jaws:* A huge man-eating shark causes fear and havoc off the east coast of the United States.

3   *Clerks:* A shop assistant is forced to work in the grocery store on his day off, which becomes filled with mishaps and idle conversations with his friend.

4   *The Toxic Avenger:* When a dim-witted weakling falls into a vat of radioactive waste, he is transformed into a deformed, mop-wielding superhero.

5   *Pi:* A mathematician seeks the answer to the meaning of the universe through analyzing numbers and Hebrew scriptures.

6   *Bugsy Malone:* A musical gangster film performed entirely by children.

7   *Toy Story:* Toys come to life when the owner is out of the room. In a fit of jealousy, one of them tries to get rid of the new toy, then has to rescue him from the sadistic kid next door.

8   *Easy Rider:* Two drop-outs ride across the country on highly customized motorbikes.

9   *Harold and Maude:* A young man, with a fixation on death and funerals, meets an 80-year-old woman at the funeral of a stranger, and they fall in love.

10   *Chicken Run:* Retelling the story of a great escape from a POW camp, starring chickens made from modeling clay.

EFFECTIVE STORYTELLING

- ▶▶ Grabbing your audience
- ▶▶ Structure: A beginning, middle, and end
- ▶▶ Structure: The hero's journey

THERE HAS BEEN LOT OF INTELLECTUAL RESEARCH INTO, AND THEORIES ABOUT, STORYTELLING, WHETHER FOR THE PRINTED PAGE OR FOR MOVING IMAGES. NOVELS AND FEATURE FILMS HAVE A CERTAIN STRUCTURE; SHORT STORIES HAVE ANOTHER.

Although some of these theories have been widely accepted and provide formulas by which the rest are judged, there is no such thing as the right way to tell a story. However, there is probably a wrong way, which will be obvious if you don't captivate your audience.

TRICKS OF THE TRADE

The trick to effective storytelling is not what you say but how you say it. A good orator can make the mundane enthralling (listen to stand-up comics such as Chris Rock or Jerry Seinfeld, for example), while a bad speaker can make capture by aliens read like a shopping list. How you tell a story will also affect how your audience interprets it. This is a common device, often used by the news media to sway people's opinions or to garner sympathy for a person or event. This is reprehensible in journalism, but it is the best tool you have in fiction.

HERO'S JOURNEY CHARACTERS ▶▶
These very basic descriptions merely outline each archetype's characteristics and roles. The subject is complex because all the archetypical traits are embodied within the human psyche. If you devise characters specifically to represent a certain archetype, remember they only play that role in relation to the hero of the story. To get a fuller understanding of mythological structure, read some of the books recommended in the Further Reading list, page 140.

THE ARCHETYPES

HERO: The protagonist, the lead character, the one whose story is being told. Heroes don't have to be good or brave (antiheroes may be neither) but they have to go on a journey— physical, emotional, or spiritual, it doesn't matter, as long as they reach their goal and have some sort of revelation.

MENTOR: A benefactor who guides the hero and imparts knowledge to them. Traditionally represented as a wise old man (Gandalf, Obi Wan Kenobi).

HERALD: The person who announces the hero or brings the message that sets the hero on the quest. Can also be a person, such as a lover, who drives the hero to do what is necessary.

In short films, as in short stories, you have to introduce your main characters in a way that allows the viewer to empathize with the protagonist, the hero, as quickly as possible, because you don't have time to divulge backstory. Equally, you have to evoke the right negative emotional response to the antagonist. Sometimes, if you are really clever, you can elicit both positive and negative feelings for a single character, depending on the individual perception of the audience. The important thing is to draw your viewer in as quickly as possible.

HOOK THEM FAST

For feature films the general consensus is that you have to grab the audience within the first ten minutes, although this really stems more from the fact that your screenplay has to hook the studio's reader within the first ten pages or it will get tossed onto the reject pile. Most audiences will sit through anything that they've had to pay for, even if it is just in anticipation of something eventually happening on screen. In short films you may not have even ten minutes in which to tell your entire story, so you need to get to the point as quickly as possible.

Short movies, like short stories, are snapshots or vignettes of a much broader story, but they are self-contained within the format. Short films have usually one act that gets to a climax and either has a surprise twist or a punch line, like a joke. They do not usually follow the same story arcs as feature films, with their three-act structure—which is not to say that they can't.

The following storytelling methods are generally used for feature-length films, but can easily be adapted to work with short films. Using them for the one- and two-minute varieties would be difficult, but even they have to have a beginning, middle and end. No matter which method you use, your story has to engage your audience, and it has to be told as concisely as possible. A short film should always be

THRESHOLD GUARDIAN: A person or an object blocking the hero's path. It can even be a subtle force such as self-doubt.

SHAPESHIFTER: Not necessarily like X-Men's Mystique or a werewolf, but a person who appears to be one type of personality but turns out to be another. The *femme fatale* is a type of shapeshifter whose beauty and charms mask something sinister.

TRICKSTER: This is the comic relief, the one who breaks the tension in the story by playing the fool or causing chaos.

SHADOW: All that is negative and has to be defeated by the hero— even if it is the hero's own neurosis. It is the dark side, as represented by Darth Vader.

as brief as you can make it, without destroying the context or flow of the story.

HOLLYWOOD FORMULA

In what has become known as the Hollywood formula, the three-act structure works as a guide to giving your film a clear beginning, middle, and end. The first act of your story introduces the characters, the premise, and the setting. This usually occupies about one-quarter of the running time. In act two (half the running time), most of the conflict and action takes place, with the third act being used to resolve the story. This is a very simplified view of the format, which needs embellishing with devices such as plot points to keep the story flowing. Conventional wisdom places these at the end of the first act, when the hero is forced into action. In the second act there is a crisis of some sort that drives the protagonist on; this can come in the middle or at the end of the act. The story then reaches a climax just before the end

of act three, where everything can be resolved to give you a Hollywood happy ending.

HERO'S JOURNEY

There is another, more complex narrative structure based on mythology, known as the hero's journey. Using the academic studies of the psychiatrist C. G. Jung and the myth theories of Joseph Campbell, this form of storytelling breaks down characters and events into archetypes. Events unfold in a prescribed sequence. This may seem like a rigid approach to storytelling, but the trick is not to use it to plan your story, but to analyze and improve it once it is written.

The best stories come, as if out of nowhere, in a flash. If you do get one of these moments of inspiration, write the story down as freely as you can, without any thought to structure or even content. Once the first draft is written, read it through and revise it into a reasonably comprehensible form.

STORYTELLING STRUCTURE ❯

The Hero's Journey and the three-act formula are staples of the Hollywood feature film factory but can be easily and successfully applied to much shorter narratives. Running at 15 minutes, *The Little Terrorist* manages to encapsulate all the steps of the mythological story structure in its story of a boy thrown into a completely different culture just a short distance from his own. (See page 10 for more about this film.)

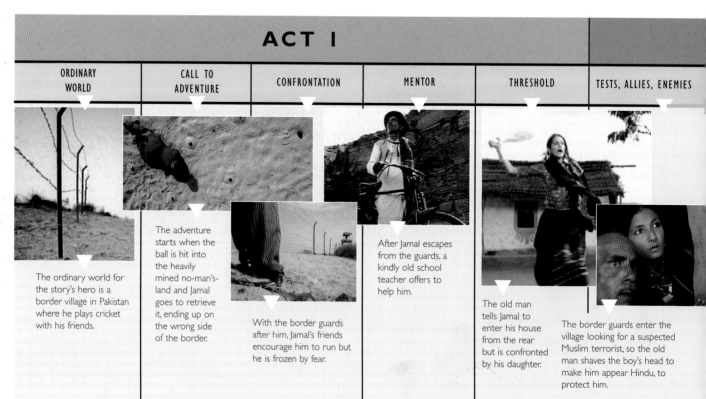

ACT I

ORDINARY WORLD	CALL TO ADVENTURE	CONFRONTATION	MENTOR	THRESHOLD	TESTS, ALLIES, ENEMIES

The ordinary world for the story's hero is a border village in Pakistan where he plays cricket with his friends.

The adventure starts when the ball is hit into the heavily mined no-man's-land and Jamal goes to retrieve it, ending up on the wrong side of the border.

With the border guards after him, Jamal's friends encourage him to run but he is frozen by fear.

After Jamal escapes from the guards, a kindly old school teacher offers to help him.

The old man tells Jamal to enter his house from the rear but is confronted by his daughter.

The border guards enter the village looking for a suspected Muslim terrorist, so the old man shaves the boy's head to make him appear Hindu, to protect him.

Now check through the list of archetypes below to see how many are present, and compare the story's structure to the Hero's Journey chart. This tends to work best within a three-act story, but you will probably find elements of it even in a short one-act story. You may even be able to fit the whole Journey into a five- or ten-minute film, but don't force it.

Many top Hollywood screenwriters and script doctors favor this mythic structure, mainly because it appeals directly to the unconscious part of our mind (many people call it the subconscious—but that is something different).

THAT'S ANOTHER STORY

As can be seen in the example below, a 15-minute film can contain all the elements of the standardized three-act mythological structure, whether it was consciously planned or not. In the current world of short movies, 15 minutes is quite long. Should you try to cram all these elements into a five-minute film? Do you need to have three acts? The answer is no.

The important thing is to convey your idea as clearly and concisely as possible. When you write your story, you have to decide: What elements do I need to tell the story and what can I leave out? I am working in a visual medium: How much of the story or characterization can I "show" rather than tell? What is the most efficient way to show it? And, how long, or short, do I have to make a shot to get the idea across?

Don't fall into the trap of thinking that short films/stories are an easy option, because they need far more careful construction than longer pieces, as demonstrated by a quote from French mathematician and physicist Blaise Pascal, who wrote as a postscript to a lengthy correspondence, "I apologize that this letter is so long—I lacked the time to make it short."

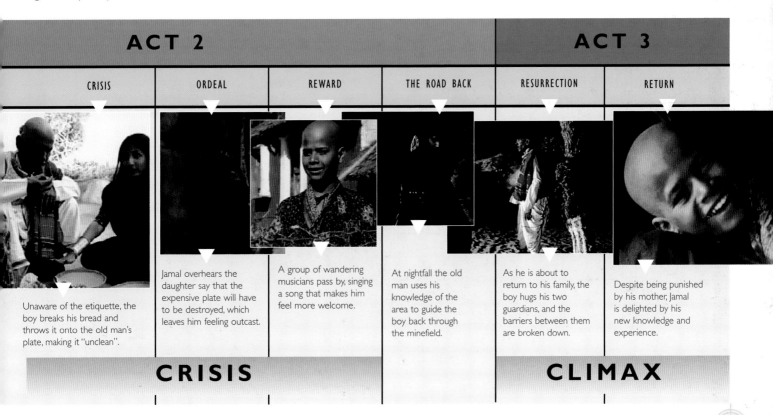

ACT 2				ACT 3	
CRISIS	ORDEAL	REWARD	THE ROAD BACK	RESURRECTION	RETURN
Unaware of the etiquette, the boy breaks his bread and throws it onto the old man's plate, making it "unclean".	Jamal overhears the daughter say that the expensive plate will have to be destroyed, which leaves him feeling outcast.	A group of wandering musicians pass by, singing a song that makes him feel more welcome.	At nightfall the old man uses his knowledge of the area to guide the boy back through the minefield.	As he is about to return to his family, the boy hugs his two guardians, and the barriers between them are broken down.	Despite being punished by his mother, Jamal is delighted by his new knowledge and experience.

CRISIS

CLIMAX

SCRIPT WRITING

ONCE YOU HAVE A STORY THAT YOU WANT TO TELL, YOU NEED TO GET IT INTO A FORMAT THAT CAN BE UNDERSTOOD AND SHARED BY EVERYONE ELSE INVOLVED IN BRINGING YOUR VISION TO FRUITION.

This is done with a screenplay or script: A document laid out in an established, industry-standard way that tells the actors what to say and the rest of the crew what to do. If only it were really that straightforward...

- ▸▸ Equipment
- ▸▸ Setting the scene
- ▸▸ Directions and dialogue

THE WRONG WAY ▸▸

A badly formatted script is very difficult to follow. The actors' dialogue disappears into the page. For the director, there are too many unnecessary camera instructions, and scene changes are too hard to find.

Camera direction is far too detailed. The writer is trying to do the director's job.

Inadequate margins, both top and bottom, and no pagination.

Prose-style scene setting is better suited to literary fiction than to film.

Rambling, long-winded camera directions lack clarity.

To avoid confusion, character names should be kept completely separate from your dialogue.

Start with black and the sound of deep breathing. Then the sound of a child shouting.

LAURA: Daaad!

Inside a bedroom in the early morning. Shoot over the shoulder of the girl with a close-up of a man's unshaven face. The girl, Laura, is lifting up one of the man's eyelids. The camera changes to what the man sees—a girl with the morning sun shining through the window highlighting her beautiful long, curly hair.

LAURA: Dad. I want my breakfast. Wide-angle shot of the bed from a higher angle. The man, Matt, rolls over, trying not to lose his eye in the process, and pulls the bedcover over his head.

MATT (in a tired, slightly jaded voice, but as a voice-over): Why is it on school days children never want to get out of bed, but come the weekend they're up before the birds?

A different wide-angle, overhead shot of the bedcover sliding down the bed and the mischievous laughter of two children. Matt sits up and looks at his peacefully sleeping wife, Ami. Would look good as a moving crane shot.

MATT (thinks in voice-over): Faker. This is my payback for all those nights of sleeping through the feeding and changing.

Matt gets out of bed, pulls the cover back over his wife, and gives her a kiss on the cheek. He turns to follow the children out of the room. Shoot it handheld and following him.

AMI (in a quiet, sleepy voice): Have a shave this morning, dear.

MATT (mumbling to himself): It's the weekend. Why do I have to shave?

New scene in the kitchen. Close up of Matt drinking a large glass of water, which pulls back to show him absentmindedly pouring cereal from a box into two bowls.

New scene of dining room. Matt places the two bowls of over-sugared cereal in front of the already overexcited children and walks toward the bathroom. Tripod shot that pans to follow the action.

New scene in bathroom. Over the shoulder, close up shots of Matt staring in the mirror. Wide angle. Lots of quick cut shots from different angles as Matt is inspecting his eyes, tongue, nose, receding hairline, and three-day stubble before lathering up and shaving.

BEGINNING

Thanks to computers, the physical act of writing a correctly formatted screenplay is relatively simple. A screenplay is just words on a page, so any word processor that applies style sheets can be adapted to the task. There are lots of formatted style sheets available on the Internet.

Your budget will probably not stretch to buying a dedicated screenplay program for your first short film. If you are shooting and directing it yourself, you can get away with not using a properly formatted script, anyway. This approach is fine while you are experimenting, but you will need to learn the correct method at some point. As your experience and ambitions grow, you may want to pitch a feature-film idea to a studio, and they won't look at anything that is not in the proper format, even down to the three screws that bind the script together.

A script that is well formatted uses typography and layout to distinguish the different script elements. Except for dialogue and a few camera directions, the text is always left-aligned. A well-formatted script doesn't need any bolds, italics, or underlining.

Simple camera directions.

e ns and ation.

A brief, correctly abbreviated set-up is all that is needed.

A clear, succinct, one-line camera direction.

The name of the character preceding the dialogue gives a clear signal to the actor of an upcoming line.

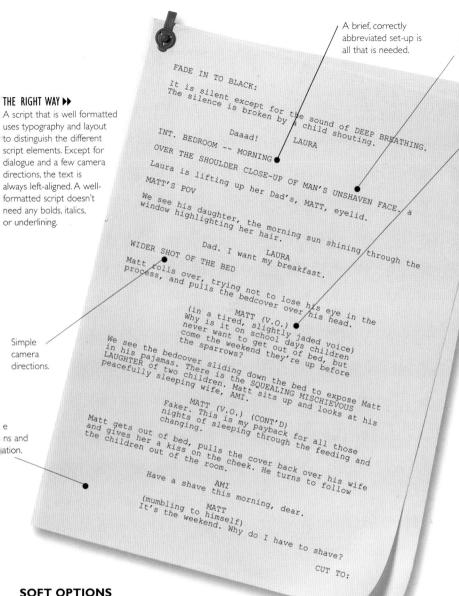

```
FADE IN TO BLACK:
It is silent except for the sound of DEEP BREATHING.
The silence is broken by a child shouting.

                    Daaad!                    LAURA
INT. BEDROOM -- MORNING
OVER THE SHOULDER CLOSE-UP OF MAN'S UNSHAVEN FACE, a
Laura is lifting up her Dad's, MATT, eyelid.
MATT'S POV
We see his daughter, the morning sun shining through the
window highlighting her hair.

                    Dad. I want my breakfast.        LAURA
WIDER SHOT OF THE BED
Matt rolls over, trying not to lose his eye in the
process, and pulls the bedcover over his head.

                    MATT (V.O.)
                (in a tired, slightly jaded voice)
            Why is it on school days children
            never want to get out of bed, but
            come the weekend they're up before
            the sparrows?
We see the bedcover sliding down the bed to expose Matt
in his pajamas. There is the SQUEALING MISCHIEVOUS
LAUGHTER of two children. Matt sits up and looks at his
peacefully sleeping wife, AMI.

                    MATT (V.O.) (CONT'D)
            Faker! This is my payback for all those
            nights of sleeping through the feeding and
            changing.
Matt gets out of bed, pulls the cover back over his wife
and gives her a kiss on the cheek. He turns to follow
the children out of the room.

                    AMI
            Have a shave this morning, dear.
                    MATT
                (mumbling to himself)
            It's the weekend. Why do I have to shave?

                                        CUT TO:
```

SOFT OPTIONS

Just about every serious screenwriter uses one of two software packages: Final Draft or Movie Magic Screenwriter. These programs format your screenplay using industry-standard layouts and terminology, keeping lists of all your characters, scenes, locations, and so on, easily accessible. They can also track your changes (and believe me, there will be plenty) in different colors. Demo versions are downloadable from the Internet. Try out both of them to decide which suits you. Once you have your software in place, you need to start writing.

FORM AND STYLE

Writing a screenplay is, in many respects, easier than writing a novel. Film is a visual medium, so all the description you need to establish mood and place in a novel is superfluous in a script. On the other hand, you still need to convey these elements to the director (if it's not you) and the actors, but in as few words as possible. For example, setting time and place is just a matter of:

    INT. COMPUTER ROOM – NIGHT
    or
    EXT. CITY STREET – MORNING

Most of us know what a city street looks like, but if there are some specifics for the scene, they can be explained—the amount of traffic, the types of buildings, and so on. These descriptions only serve as notes or reminders. If you are writing a spec script, keep it as generic as possible, unless of course you need to set the story in a specific city. New York and Kathmandu are both cities, but that is about all they have in common. With your low-budget script, the city will no doubt refer to your local area.

When describing a character's appearance, you can be equally vague, unless there is a specific, physically defining trait. Sometimes using an existing film character or actor as an example is enough. If you write "a Humphrey Bogart–type character," everyone will know exactly what you mean. There is also no harm in having a fantasy cast list or writing with a specific actor in mind. For your first movies, your actors will quite possibly be people you already know, but you never can predict your luck.

GIVING DIRECTIONS

It is advisable not to put too many directorial and camera instructions in the script. If the screenplay is for another director, the instructions will usually be ignored. If you are directing it yourself, you already know exactly what you want to do; these ideas are best put on the storyboards. When writing scene descriptions and actions, always use the present tense.

Apart from the brief scene setting and descriptions of action, the bulk of your script is going to be dialogue. This is invariably the hardest part to write, as you have to play each character's role in your head, so that all the dialogue doesn't come out in the same "voice" or, worse, clichéd.

One of the generally accepted rules of script writing is that one page of properly formatted screenplay equals one minute of screen time. However, this tends to apply more accurately to a feature film of 90 minutes or more, where dialogue and action balance out. It is possible for the screenplay for a five-minute film to be one page and that for a one-minute film to be several pages.

Once you've written the script and revised it to a state with which you are happy, get some actors to read it for you. It's not until you hear your dialogue spoken that you will really know if it works. Let the actors give you their feedback, take notes of what they say, whether you agree or not, and thank them. By reading the script for you they have already done you a service, so there is no need to get into a debate with them. Take your notes from the reading and make whatever revisions you feel the script needs. Then you're ready to move on to the next stage.

CHECK THESE OUT

www.finaldraft.com Web site for Final Draft software

www.screenplay.com Web site for Movie Magic Screenwriter software

www.simplyscripts.com Links to free, downloadable movie scripts

www.screentalk.biz Web site of the magazine "Screentalk"

www.thesws.com Web site of the Screenwriters' Store, selling books and software for screenwriters and filmmakers

CREATING A STYLE SHEET ⯯

If you don't want to buy dedicated screenwriting software, you can easily create style sheets in your favorite word processing program. This example shows how to do it in Microsoft Word, but the settings are the same for all programs.

Start by setting measurements to inches in the general preferences, then setting your Document Margins to Left: 0", Right: 0", Top: 0.3", and Bottom: 0.8".

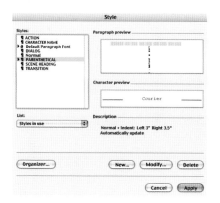

1 ⯭
From the Format menu, select Style, and select New from the window.

SETTING OUT THE SCREENPLAY ⯯
Most commonly used styles for screenplays and the settings required.

2 ⯭
From the Format button, now select Paragraph and enter the relevant Indent settings as listed below. All screenplays have Single Line spacing.

Name	Font style	Left margin	Right margin	Space before	Indent	Para after
Character name	All Caps	3.7"	1"	12pt		Dialogue
Dialogue		2.5"	2.4"			Action
Parentheticals		3"	3.5"		0.1"	Dialogue
Scene headings	All Caps	1.5"	1"	12pt		Action
Shots	All Caps	1.5"	1"	12pt		Action
Action		1.5"	1"	12pt		
Transitions	All Caps	1.5"	1"	12pt	Flush right	Action
Act information	All Caps	1.5"	1"	12pt	Center	
Scene information	All Caps	1.5"	1"	12pt	Center	

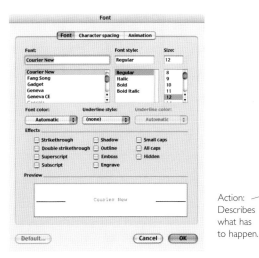

3 ▲
All screenplays are written in 12 point Courier New. Some styles utilize All·Caps, which can be set here.

4 ▲
Name the style and, from the pop-up Format button at the bottom of the window, select Font. Once you have built all the Styles, you can go back and modify them to incorporate the "Style for following paragraph" option.

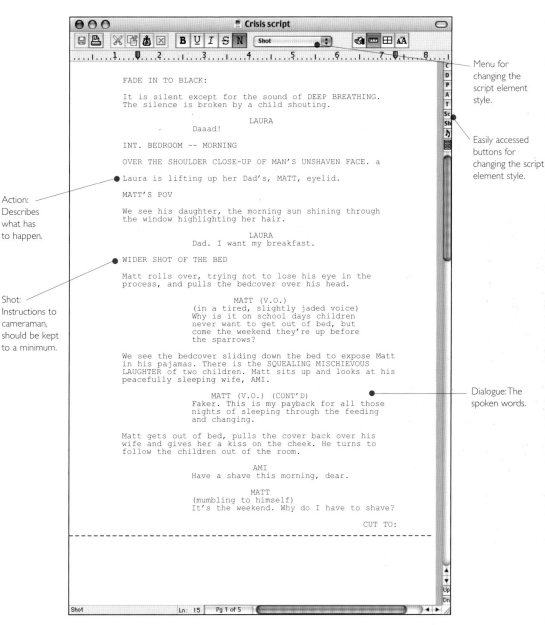

Menu for changing the script element style.

Easily accessed buttons for changing the script element style.

Action: Describes what has to happen.

Shot: Instructions to cameraman, should be kept to a minimum.

Dialogue: The spoken words.

SCREENWRITING AIDS ▲
Screenwriting software programs are specialized word processors with features to assist with the layout and editing of the screenplay. They can also break down scripts for scheduling. This is a working page from Movie Magic Screenwriter 2000.

STORYBOARDS

THE SCRIPT IS THE WRITTEN BLUEPRINT FOR YOUR MOVIE, AND THE STORYBOARD IS THE VISUAL GUIDE. SCREENPLAYS ARE BEST PRESENTED IN THE CORRECT STANDARDIZED FORMAT, BUT STORYBOARDS AREN'T NECESSARILY PLACED UNDER SUCH RIGID CONSTRAINTS.

▸▸ Explaining concepts

▸▸ Make sure the film works

▸▸ Storyboard formats

HAND-DRAWN STORYBOARDS ⬇

Create a series of screen ratio boxes on your computer and print them. Then, sketch in the shots with any notes you might want. The drawings don't need to be elaborate—they're simply to remind you what you want to shoot.

Each director has his or her own approach to storyboards, from highly detailed drawings of every shot to simple napkin scribbles of the most complex scenes. How you use storyboards will depend on your experience and working methods.

WHY STORYBOARDS?

One of the primary reasons for using storyboards is to convey your ideas to other members of the production team, especially the DoP (cinematographer or cameraman). It may also be useful for explaining concepts to the visually illiterate, such as some producers and money people. When the Wachowski Brothers were trying to get *The Matrix* made, they had to get elaborate storyboards drawn because the people who could greenlight the project didn't understand the script.

Although it is not necessary to storyboard every shot, having a detailed storyboard can make the shoot run a lot more smoothly. It does not mean that you have to adhere rigidly to what you've drawn, because unexpected things will happen during the shoot, or someone, including you, may come up with a better idea. In these situations, if you aren't flexible you will probably end up going crazy or missing a special, magical shot.

SETTING THE PACE

A storyboard is useful in preproduction for checking the flow and pacing of the story. This can be done with an animatic, which involves making a video of the storyboards and adding the dialogue from the script. You can either shoot each storyboard frame to the requisite length with your video camera, or use a scanner and edit the images together on your computer, dubbing the sound on later. The animatic will give you a good idea of the film's running time, and any superfluous scenes or shots will become immediately evident.

For short films, where time is at a premium, storyboards and animatics will help in ensuring that the film works. Editing a feature film to a manageable length is a matter of cutting minutes at a time from it, but when you are only working with minutes, you have to make the most of every second.

In traditional animated films, storyboarding is a vital stage because you don't have the luxury of retakes or reshoots. Experimenting with different angles is not a viable option when there are thousands of drawings involved. 3D CGI (computer-generated images)

SCENE 1 - BALLOON

animation does offer more flexibility to experiment before the final render, but it is still a time- and labor-intensive activity. Shooting live action, on the other hand, especially on video, does afford you the luxury of multiple takes, which can ultimately be resolved in the editing suite—usually.

DETAILS

As storyboards are visual reminders, how detailed you make them is entirely up to you. Plain white record cards are an ideal medium; they are also useful when developing your script. You can make your sketches on one side and write notes on the other. Cards can be pinned to a wall or notice board (which is where the name storyboard comes from), and are easily shuffled about. Alternatively, you can draw some boxes to your screen ratio and print them from your computer, or photocopy them. These sheets can be bound into a folder, to avoid losing them. Don't worry if you can't draw, because the quality of the pictures is not that important: even stick figures will do, as long as the idea is conveyed.

GOING DIGITAL

Naturally, in this digital age, there are software solutions too. Two companies are competing for the

Overview of the set/location layout

Preview of shot, showing tracking shot framing

Controls for altering the pose of the character

Preview of character pose to check as adjustments are made

Camera movement controls

Library of actors and props

STORYBOARD SOFTWARE ⬆

Storyboard software doesn't come more comprehensive than FrameForge 3D. A huge library of 3D characters, props, and locations enables you to create a mini version of your movie and try out camera angles, movements, and lenses.

Characters can be posed into any position and the script imported to let you create "animatics" to test your film before taking any shots. The risk is that you will spend more time creating the storyboard than actually shooting the film.

market share (much as in scriptwriting): Power Productions' Storyboard programs, which come in three versions—Storyboard Quick, Storyboard Artist, and Storyboard Artist Pro—each with an increasingly complex range of features, and FrameForge 3D.

All these programs let you create storyboards from libraries of scenes, props, and characters, or you can add your own digital photos of locations. Some can integrate with scriptwriting software and also produce animatics, so you can have a clear idea during pre-production of how your movie should work. These programs produce rather generic results that lack the charm of hand-drawn boards, but they are reasonably economical, quick, and easily edited, which makes them worth considering as an option.

Whichever method you choose, storyboards are a vital part of the production process. They will make your work, and that of others, much easier, no matter which role(s) in the production you choose.

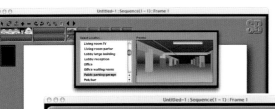

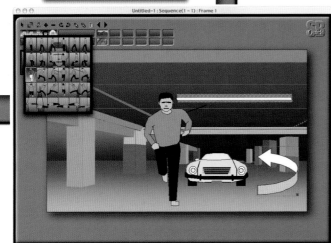

STORYBOARD QUICK ◀◀

Storyboard Quick is a simple 2D storyboard software. It is fast and easy to use, although the generic look and limited poses will not suit everyone. Digital shots of your locations can be imported to get a better feeling for the production.

THE BUDGET

MONEY MAKES THE WORLD GO ROUND, AS THE SAYING GOES, AND WHEN IT COMES TO MAKING MOVIES IT SEEMS TO BE A MAJOR CRITERION. IN HOLLYWOOD, A MOVIE'S MERITS ARE JUDGED BY ITS FINANCES: "THIS FILM COST $100 MILLION TO MAKE"; "THAT FILM GROSSED $100 MILLION AT THE BOX OFFICE" (OF COURSE, IF IT WAS THE SAME FILM, IT ACTUALLY LOST MONEY).

▸▸ Do your research

▸▸ Factor in all expenses

Then there is the other extreme, which usually applies to first-time indy films, where there seems to be competition based on how little it cost to shoot (such as the $7,000 it cost to make *El Mariachi*). These are the positive spins. The negative production comments usually tend to revolve around how much over-budget a movie went. So how do you avoid this?

One way is simply not to discuss the budget with anyone. This could be tricky if someone else is funding your film. Naturally, they will want to know where their money is going, or went. Chances are, for your first films you will have no funding, personal or otherwise, and, although it is possible to make a movie for almost no money, drawing up a hypothetical budget is an excellent exercise.

One reason to start with short films is to learn as much as possible about all aspects of the filmmaking process, and drawing up a budget is something that will help prevent you from being ripped off in the future. If you know how much everything costs, you are not going to be tricked into paying more than you should.

BE ACCOUNTABLE

It is best to set up your budget using a computer spreadsheet. It doesn't have to be very complex: one column for the names of items, one for their list prices, a column for what you expect to pay, and, most importantly, one for what you actually paid.

Your first unavoidable expenses are going to be equipment and consumables. The question of rental or purchase has already been covered, but you should factor in a cost even if you purchased your camera. If you are using film, at some time you are going to have to pay for it, no matter how good your haggling skills are, and it is going to cost a lot more than DV tape.

The other inescapable cost is your talent (the actors) and the crew. Even if they are working for nothing, you have to pay their travel expenses and feed them (see pages 80–81). Find out what the minimum union rates are for the people you are using, and include it in your budget. The normal cost of time or services when donated is usually known as payment in kind. This can be very useful if you ever want to apply for a grant or other non-commercial funding, as it counts as part of your financial contribution to a project.

Other expenses to factor in are props, costumes, makeup, lighting, transportation, and location and studio fees. The list goes on and on. For your first films, you will probably be getting these for nothing, but as you become more professional, every aspect of the production has to be accounted for. It is worth getting into the habit of accounting for everything while it is easy. When you start on properly financed films, all these items become deductible expenses, so always keep receipts.

And if you find the thought of doing all this number crunching a bit daunting, find someone else to do it for you. Remember that they too become a deductible expense.

SAMPLE BUDGET ▼

Even no-budget filmmaking incurs expenses, and while it may be possible to eliminate most of these by getting the cast and crew to pay their own way, it is not the best idea if you want to work with them again. This budget is for a ten-minute film shot on miniDV with four actors and four crew over three days, and came to $300.

Finding cast and crew was done using a filmmakers' Internet bulletin.

A local amateur theater hired out one of their spare rooms for auditions.

Auditions had to be videotaped to help with selections.

Camera and sound equipment was borrowed. No extra artificial light was needed.

Feeding the cast and crew is important and need not be expensive (see Catering, pages 80–81).

Some cash for emergencies.

Apart from feeding the cast and crew, paying their travel expenses is the least you can do. Allow the same for everyone even if they choose to walk or cycle, but make sure they live locally to keep the cost down. Actor 1 "donated" his car as a prop so he received a little extra for fuel.

The formula needed to create the total of the line of each item.

Item	Quantity	Unit cost	Total	Notes
PRE-PRODUCTION				
Advertising for cast and crew	1	0.00	0.00	
Audition space per day	2	10.00	20.00	
Tapes for audition	3	2.00	6.00	
PRODUCTION				
Camera rental	1	0.00	0.00	
Microphone rental	1	0.00	0.00	
Light rental	0	0.00	0.00	
DV tape stock	3	2.00	6.00	
Script	10	0.50	5.00	
Photocopies				
Props	3	5.00	15.00	Toy guns
Wardrobe	0	0.00	0.00	
Makeup	1	5.00	5.00	Fake blood
Catering for 8 per day	3	20.00	60.00	
Petty cash			20.00	
TRAVEL EXPENSES PER DAY				
Actor 1	3	7.00	21.00	Includes gas for car used in movie
Actor 2	3	5.00	15.00	
Actor 3	3	5.00	15.00	
Actor 4	3	5.00	15.00	
Cameraman	3	5.00	15.00	
Sound recordist	3	5.00	15.00	
Makeup	3	5.00	15.00	
Director	3	5.00	15.00	
POST-PRODUCTION				
Editor	1	0.00	0.00	
DVD-R	20	1.00	20.00	For cast, crew, and marketing
Marketing/PR	10	2.00	20.00	Printing press pack
Total			**303.00**	

Supplying a copy of the finished film to all the participants is vital as they can use it for their audition tapes.

Even using your own printer at home will need ink and paper.

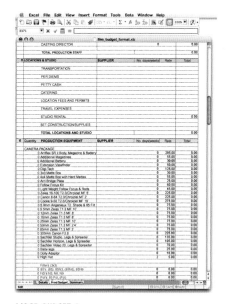

LARGE BUDGET ▲

An Excel spreadsheet template for a large budget film shoot, listing all the items you could ever need to purchase. This is available to download from www.shootingpeople.org.

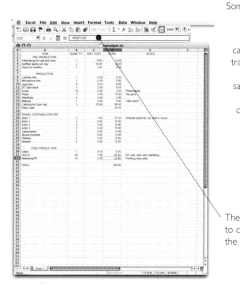

SMALL BUDGET (ENLARGED AT RIGHT) ▲

Using a spreadsheet such as Microsoft Excel is the easiest way to produce a budget. You can add an extra column for actual expenses, taken from your receipts, if you want to compare them with your projected costs.

CHOOSING A CREW

ALTHOUGH ITS SIZE DEPENDS ON THE COMPLEXITY OF YOUR SCREENPLAY, YOU ARE GOING TO NEED A CREW WITH THE SPECIALIZED SKILLS TO HELP YOU REALIZE YOUR PROJECT.

- ▸▸ Less is more
- ▸▸ Multitasking
- ▸▸ Who does what?

At the lo-no budget end of moviemaking, the fewer people you have working for you the better. This is primarily an economic consideration because, even if you aren't paying them, you have to at least feed them and cover their travel expenses.

If you can convince friends to help out willingly, without so much as a sandwich in recompense, that is another matter—and if they volunteer to work under those terms, better still. Of course, you don't want to surround yourself with deadwood either. When shooting guerrilla-style, you will need a small, tight-knit, multitasking crew that can work fast, anticipate situations, and solve problems.

As the size of the budget increases, so does the crew—and vice versa. You only have to watch the credits on a feature film to see the huge number of assistants, and assistants to the assistants, and so on *ad infinitum*. On small films it is best to get people each to do a variety of tasks—it is good experience for them and it makes for a tighter, more manageable team. Too much specialization results in an incredible amount of standing around on film sets, and if people are not busy they want to eat—or talk. The busier everyone is, the more they will enjoy it and the greater their sense of achievement.

When you pick your crew, start with friends, or friends of friends. Acquaintance helps break the ice, and has the added advantage of recommendation, which isn't always a guarantee of ability. An alternative is to join a local theater group, which will give you access to all sorts of resources and skills that can easily be translated to movies. Only get people to do the jobs you can't actually do yourself, physically or

technically. This is your show, so try to do as much as possible; but once you do take someone on, let them get on with their job—providing they are not messing up. The important things to get across are first, that you are in charge, and second, that you appreciate their help. Praise and thanks go a long way when there's no money.

In the coming pages, the various jobs will be covered in more detail, giving you a better idea of what is needed so that you can decide on the ideal size of crew for your project.

HOW MANY MAKE A CREW? ▸▸

It is possible to make a film on your own (depending on how you intend to capture the sound), but that degree of autonomy is not always a good idea. The best plan is to go through the jobs listed and decide which ones you can do yourself, which you can delegate, and which will need someone with experience to advise and assist.

PRODUCER

The producer runs practically everything, particularly the money side, and is the business face of the film. He or she usually comes from one of two angles. Either he or she has an idea for a film, or likes the idea of making a film, and hires all the necessary talent to bring it to fruition; or a writer/director wants to make a film and needs someone to take care of the business end, leaving him or her free to be creative. If you have good business sense and like dealing with all sorts of people, you should be able to take on the producer's role. The person who takes care of the day-to-day running of the picture is called the line producer.

DIRECTOR

Directing is perceived to be the glamor job. The director is ultimately responsible for the look and feel of the movie. The ideal is to be a writer/director, because this way the creative vision is taken from conception to completion. A lot of the director's work is organizational, ensuring that everything is ready for the shoot and is in the right place when "action" is called. Depending on his or her strengths, the director may take on many roles, but in indy films (at least) the director is the boss, as long as he stays on budget. A good director needs to be a visionary ... and somewhat of a control freak.

DIRECTOR OF PHOTOGRAPHY (DoP)

The director of photography, or cinematographer, has the job of capturing the images to match the director's vision. More than just a camera operator, he or she has to work with the director on deciding the best angles, lighting, lenses, camera movements, and so on. If, as the director, you don't feel technically confident, an experienced DoP will make a huge difference to the final look of your film. Nevertheless, learn to operate your own camera.

ASSISTANT DIRECTOR (AD)

Assistant directors are the eyes, ears, and especially the mouth of the director. They are indispensable on large sets because they do all the dull (but necessary) work, while the director is occupied with the "vision." They are superfluous on a small shoot.

CAMERA ASSISTANT ◀◀

An important job on a film shoot is "checking the gate," usually carried out by the camera assistant. This means ensuring that no hair, dust, or other matter is present that can mar the film as it passes the shutter. This issue does not affect video.

SOUND RECORDIST/ BOOM OPERATOR

If you are shooting on film, and unless you are making a silent or dialogue-free film or a pop video, you will need a sound recordist. You won't need one if you are working with video, but you will need a boom operator. The boom operator is a person of great stamina and strength who has to hold a long pole with attached microphone over his or her head during a take, keeping it out of the frame but as close as possible to the actors. Not as easy as it sounds. A vital crew member.

CONTINUITY PERSON/ SCRIPT SUPERVISOR

After the director, the continuity person has perhaps the most important role on the set; his or her effectiveness prevents your film from turning up on one of those movie-mistakes TV shows. Their job is to make sure that everything matches up from shot to shot and take to take. A meticulous eye for detail, verging on the obsessive, is imperative. A digital still camera makes the job easier, but it is no substitute for observation.

PRODUCTION ASSISTANT (PA)

Perhaps the busiest members of the crew, the production assistants have to organize everything and make it happen. The AD is involved in the actual shoot, but the PA has to oversee all the practical aspects of the film, making sure everyone and everything are where they should be, and as cheaply as possible.

PRODUCTION DESIGNER/ART DIRECTOR

The production designer is responsible for creating the look of the sets and getting them made, found, or bought. Get them to work with the PA on sorting out props, etc. (see pages 46–47).

COSTUME AND MAKEUP

Costume and makeup must make the talent look the part. Although the stars have to shine, makeup has to take away the sheen (see pages 48–49).

GRIP

Grips handle the equipment that lets the camera move—dolly, crane, etc. If you have that sort of equipment, you will need someone to operate it. Getting smooth dolly or track shots isn't as easy as you think.

EDITOR

Although the editing comes after the shoot, it is advisable to get the editor involved as early as possible. A good editor can make your picture … and a bad one can ruin it. An experienced editor can give you invaluable advice about what to shoot (coverage) so that they have plenty of material to work with. (See pages 86–91.)

EXTRA CREW

Gaffer: Chief electrician, responsible for lights. AKA "sparks."

Best boy: Gaffer's assistant.

Focus puller: Adjusts focus during filming.

Clapper loader: Writes details on clapperboard/slate.

Grip: Person who transports and sets up equipment and props. Operates equipment such as the dolly.

Key grip: In charge of grips.

Swing gang: People who set up and dismantle the sets.

Location manager: Books and oversees location shoots. Gets permits.

Runner: Runs, or drives, around delivering messages, cast, crew, or collecting props. Does anything no one else wants to. Paid slave wages.

Steadicam operator: Operates Steadicam— usually a specially trained camera person.

CLAPPER LOADER ▲

CASTING AND REHEARSALS

ASSUMING THAT YOUR FORAY INTO SHORT FILMS IS NEITHER A DOCUMENTARY NOR ANIMATION, YOU ARE GOING TO NEED SOME ACTORS (OR "TALENT"). FINDING A COMPETENT, EXPERIENCED CREW (WHOM YOU DON'T KNOW), WILLING TO WORK FOR NOTHING, IS DIFFICULT—MAINLY BECAUSE IF THEY ARE ANY GOOD, THEY ARE ALREADY EARNING A LIVING.

- ▶▶ Sourcing talent
- ▶▶ Audition protocol
- ▶▶ Rehearsing

On the other hand, competition among actors for the few paying roles is fierce. When actors say "break a leg" to each other, they mean it. Most actors "between jobs" will be happy for the chance to appear in low-budget films, even without payment, because it will give them material for their résumés. Of course, it is up to you to make it something they would want to include.

So how do you go about finding actors who are between jobs?

CASTING ON THE NET

There are Web sites, such as shootingpeople.org, that run daily bulletins for actors and filmmakers.

TALENT ON THE WEB ▶▶
With a little research, you can find all the talent resources you need. Many Web sites have links to talented actors looking for work. Some may even consider acting in low- or no-budget productions on which they can cut their teeth.

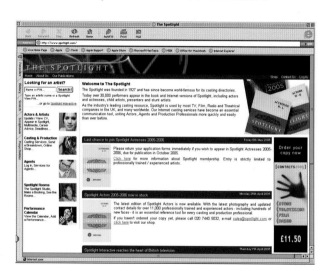

Subscribers to the site can display a card outlining their skills, experience, and other personal data. This makes it an excellent starting point, especially as subscribers are already in the lo-no budget mindset.

Another excellent resource, already mentioned, is a local theater group or theater workshop. Signing up to take part in actors' workshops is a good way to meet actors, and learning some basic acting skills and techniques will help you as a director. If you understand, first hand, the acting process you will be able not only to relate to the talent but also to coax better performances from them. Acting for theater and film are two slightly different disciplines. Film requires short bursts of acting, often understated, that may have to be repeated several times in a short space of time, whereas the stage needs sustained and "large," almost exaggerated, performances. Film acting is more intimate, as you are performing to a very small audience that scrutinizes your every word and movement. Some stage actors have problems adapting to film because they are too theatrical, an approach that appears unnatural on camera. It is therefore very important to have auditions.

AUDITIONING

Your initial selection will be based on physical attributes, and is usually made from the glossy pictures that actors send out. As they show only one pose, and are designed to represent the actor at his or her

Diane Elmsworth

108 The High Street, London N23 7ST
Phone: 020 8667 4437. Mobile: 07489 400 099
E-mail: dielmsworth@hotmail.com
Agent: Bruce Palmer Associates, London 020 7601 7777

Equity No. 00379545
Height: 5' 2" **Weight:** 110 lb
Hair: Red/brown **Eyes:** Blue

Training

- Italia Conti 3 year Performing Arts Course (majoring in drama), ALAM (Hons) & LLAM diplomas
- Camera Acting Technique at the Studio on the Drive & UBCP, Vancouver, BC
- Physical Theatre skills with Rough Cut Theatre Co.
- Classical Indian Singing – Nagpur Academy of Arts, India
- Also private lessons with Shweta Jhaveri, Berkeley, CA
- Jazz/rhythm tap (with Tobias Tak and Derek Hartley)
- 'Hoofin' (with Brock Jellison), Vancouver, BC

Skills

- **Voice:** Soprano with good low-mid range (low Db to F in alto). Good music sight-reader.
- **Other:** Singer/songwriter – performs and records own material. Plays guitar and drums.
- Good ear for dialects/accents (esp. Australia, NZ, South Africa, US, Irish, Welsh, and English regional).
- Certified PADI Open Water Scuba Diver; can rollerblade, ice skate, ride a horse, drive a car and motorbike.
- Will not do nude scenes.
- Can play ages from late teens upwards.

Experience

Theatre: roles include:

Dregs the Musical (workshop)	Ensemble	Arts Club Revue Theatre, Vancouver BC
Relative Values (Noel Coward)	Alice	Metro Theatre, Vancouver BC
Music of Life Gala	Ensemble	Palace Theatre, London, Dir. Simon Callow
Le Malade Imaginaire (Molière)	Louison	Edinburgh Fringe Festival, Europe & India tours
A Crucial Week in the Life of a Grocer's Assistant		Edinburgh Fringe Festival
Tosca	Mona	Earls Court, Dir. Francessca Zambello
Beauty & the Beast	Ensemble	Questors Theatre, London
	Beauty	

Cabaret/Singing:

- **Performing own material** – many **London** venues, inc 12 Bar Club, Rock Garden, Hope & Anchor and The Borderline; **LA** - Kulak's Woodshed, Taxi Lounge, Canter's Kibbitz Room; **Vancouver**, BC – CBC studios for Alibi Unplugged.
- **Featuring own material** – Soundtrack for *Manji* – short film (UK release), soundtrack for *Happy Now* – feature film (UK release), several independent compilation CDs.
- **Jazz/blues trio** "Realisation" – London wine bars/cafes
- **Ambrosian Chorus** – Soundtrack - *Santa Claus the Movie* & recording of Tchaikovsky's *The Nutcracker*

TV/Film:
Many major London-based productions including:
EASTENDERS for BBC TV. **THE BILL** for Carlton TV.
JUDGE JOHN DEED for BBC TV. **HOLBY CITY** for BBC TV.

BEDAZZLED for Apple Pie Productions. **THE JACKAL** for Jackal Productions Ltd.
FIRST KNIGHT for First Knight Productions Ltd. **MARY SHELLEY'S FRANKENSTEIN**
for Shepperton Productions Ltd. **FOUR WEDDINGS & A FUNERAL** for Four Weddings Ltd.

Also:
Independent Canadian Feature: **SISTERS** for Blue Media Inc.

most glamorous, these are not always helpful. Always look at the actor's height. Unless you specifically need big differences, trying to frame very tall and very short people in the same shot can be difficult.

Once you have chosen the actors you want to audition, make very clear to them any special demands you will be making—nudity, equestrian skills, working at heights—anything that is out of the ordinary. For paying jobs, actors will often lie to get the part, but with freebies, impress upon them the importance of being honest, as you don't want to jeopardize them or the shoot. You will also need to know their availability.

For the auditions, find neutral territory and avoid private homes. A local theater may have a space you can use, which will also be useful for rehearsals.

During auditions it is a good idea to have someone of the opposite sex in the room to remove any possibility, or accusations, of impropriety. Having an actor with you to read any other roles is useful, as is someone to operate a video camera. Always get the actors to give their name at the beginning of the audition so you know who they are when you play the tape back.

There are many different approaches to auditioning. Some directors like to give the actors a script so they can prepare, while others like them to sight-read. You have to decide which method will give you the results you need to make the right decision.

After the initial audition, draw up a short list of the people you want to see again. Get them to perform with other actors you have chosen. The intangible and mysterious "chemistry" between performers does exist, and you need to do your best to find it, or at least something close.

AUDITION ETIQUETTE

Apart from ensuring that there is at least one person of each sex present, there are levels of courtesy toward the actors that you should observe. Always thank them for coming, be enthusiastic but professional about their performance, no matter how good or bad—this isn't *American Idol*. If they have come from an agent, tell them you will let their agent know, otherwise you have the thankless task of letting

AUDITION TEST PIECES

To make the most of an audition, you should test the actor's skills and ability to get into character. Using these four methods should give you a good idea of what the actor is capable of.

1   Send the actors a script and ask them to learn a designated passage for the audition. Alternatively, just send them one scene to learn, to see how they interpret the character from that scene. The piece should be from the script you intend to shoot. This will test their understanding of the character and their ability to memorize lines.

2   At the audition, give them an unseen piece, either of the same character or another character they might be suitable to play. Get them to read it through without preparation. When they have finished, get them to read it but with direction. This will test how quickly they can get into character and take direction.

3   Discuss a possible back-story of the character with the actor and get him or her to improvise a scene, with another actor, that leads up to the one just performed or read. After the improvisation, get them to redo the scripted piece. This will test their ability to get into character and how they can contribute to the role.

4   If there are any scenes that require special skills or handling of specific props, they should be performed for the camera.

them know that they have not been successful. Don't do this until you have your cast firmly agreed; it is not very good to tell someone they haven't got the part, only to have to call them later to say they have. If your first choice can't do it, offer the part to your next choice, and so on until you have someone. Never reveal they weren't your first choice. Give all the actors a deadline for letting them know, and always tell them either way. E-mail or text are the coward's ways out—apologize for using them by saying the number of people who auditioned did not permit personal calls. Remember that, unless they are complete novices, the actors have heard it all before.

YOU (ALMOST) GOT THE JOB ▶▶

These are letters for the actors that almost made it or who you liked enough to try to fit them in elsewhere. It's quite certain that you'll want to see them again. Keep the lines of communication open and you'll always have a great pool of talent to choose from in the future.

Dear [Actor]

Thank you for taking the time to attend the audition for our movie [Insert Title]. Your interpretation of the character was both original and enthusiastic. We saw a lot of actors and, after much deliberation, have given the part to someone who better fits our overall vision.

We would, however, like to offer you the part of [another character] for which we think you would be perfect. If you would like this role, then please let me know by email: producer@lonofilms.com as soon as possible, as the shooting date is fast approaching. Thank you again, and I hope to hear from you very soon.

Producer
Lono Films

Dear [Actor]

Thank you for taking the time to attend the audition for our movie [Insert Title]. Your interpretation of the character was both original and enthusiastic. I apologize for not having the time to call you personally, but we saw a lot of actors and, after much deliberation, have given the part to someone who better fits our overall vision.

We would like to keep your details on our records, for future productions and to share with other filmmakers we are associated with. If you have any objections to this, then please let me know by email: producer@lonofilms.com Thank you again for your time, and best wishes for future auditions.

Producer
Lono Films

DON'T CALL US! ◀◀

When composing a rejection letter, remember to keep it tactful and encouraging. You never know—the actor you disliked today might be perfect for a future production. Don't create enemies.

REHEARSALS

Even with a five- or ten-minute film, you are going to need some rehearsals. The actors will need to get a handle on their characters and establish a rapport with the rest of the cast. You may need only a couple of days, but even that will help when it comes to the shoot. It will also give you an idea of how you might want to alter the shoot to suit the talent.

As director, you must know what you are looking for in the performances. Because short films are often just snapshots from an ongoing story, you need to have a clear idea of the background and work through this with the actors. The genre and the script will dictate the nature of the rehearsals. An action piece will require one sort of rehearsal, a dialogue-heavy drama will need another. Let the actors feed you ideas; just remember who is in charge.

Cast well, rehearse well, and your shoot should go smoothly—or at least more smoothly than if you had cut corners. Rehearsals ultimately save time and money.

SHOT LIST AND SCHEDULE

DRAWING UP A SHOOTING SCHEDULE WILL MAKE THE MANAGEMENT OF YOUR SHOOT RUN A LOT MORE SMOOTHLY. THE LARGER THE PRODUCTION, THE MORE VITAL PROPER SCHEDULING BECOMES.

- » The logistics
- » Useful computer software
- » Be realistic

Shooting a one- or two-minute movie with one or two actors in a single setting will not necessarily benefit from, or even require, the same degree of planning, but once you move to multiple settings, locations, and actors, logistics demand it.

The main reason for having a shooting schedule is that of economics. Even if there is no money involved, there are the economics of time. Without a properly coordinated schedule, you are going to waste a lot of time, which can lead to frayed tempers and even missed shots. For example, if you have a location that is only available for one day but appears at different times in the script, you have to shoot everything on that day with all the right costumes, props, and actors —and the all-important continuity person noting every detail.

SCHEDULING SOFTWARE ⩢

Scheduling and production software, such as GorillaPro, makes organizing a shoot much easier, especially for feature films. The time it saves is worth the cost.

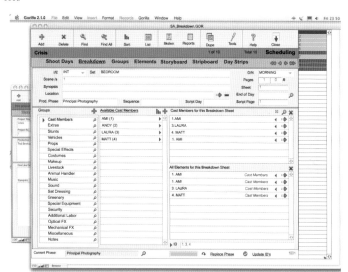

SHOOTING SCHEDULE ⩢

Breaking down the schedule into separate parts, so you know who and what needs to be where, will make your job that much easier. A table like this can easily be created in Microsoft Word or Excel.

SHOOTING DAY — DAY 1 (Scenes 1–7) · DAY 2 (Scenes 6, 8, 9)

TITLE: Crisis
DIRECTOR: Alan Smithee
DOP: Mario Chiaroscuro
AD: Anna Nuddating

	Matt's Bedroom	Matt's Kitchen	Matt's Dining Room	Matt's Bathroom	Matt's Dining Room	Busy Road	Parking Lot	Busy Road	Parking Lot	Car
LOCATION / STUDIO	L	L	L	L	L	L	L	L	L	L
INT / EXT	I	I	I	I	I	E	I	E	E	I
DAY / NIGHT	D	D	D	D	D	D	D	D	D	D
SCENE NUMBER	1	2	3	4	5	6	7	6	8	9
PAGE COUNT	8/8	1/8	1/8	3/8	7/8	1/8	1/8	1/8	2/8	8/8
CAST:										
Actor 1: Matt	1	1	1	1	1	1	1	1	1	1
Actor 2: Ami	2			2	2	2	2	2	2	2
Actor 3: Laura	3		3		3	3	3	3	3	3
Actor 4: Andy	4		4		4	4	4	4	4	4
Actor 5: Pedestrian						5				
PROPS:										
Cereal (C)		C	C							
Shaving gear (S)				S						
Newspaper (N)			N							
MPV (M)						M	M	M	M	M
Child car seats (CS)						CS	CS	CS	CS	CS
CAMERA EQUIPMENT:										
Steadicam (SC)	SC	SC	SC	SC						SC
Car Mount (CM)								CM		CM
Crane (CR)									CR	

BREAKING DOWN THE SCRIPT

To start your list you will need to break the script down into its basic constituent parts—scenes, locations, actors—but also keep note of shot length (this is done by dividing the script page into eighths and marking how many eighths a scene requires), props, effects, and camera equipment. The best way to start is by writing everything on scene cards, made from index file cards. Once you have broken down all the scenes, you have to start adding in the variables.

Factors to consider include: distances between locations; which are day or night shots; interior or exterior; when locations are available. Then you have to factor in the actors: which days they are available; who is appearing with whom; the list goes on. Then you have to make it all coalesce.

Computers are ideal for calculating this, especially if there are lots of combinations and variations. Dedicated software such as MovieMagic Scheduling or Gorilla can import a correctly formatted file from your screenwriting software and break it down for you. These are professional programs that incorporate a huge range of production and budgeting tools, but they come with a professional price tag. Spreadsheets or databases with variable sorting are options, if you know how to use them, or you'll have to settle for shuffling bits of paper around by hand.

When you've finished your calculations, you will have a sheet of paper, or better still a board, divided into days, with locations/sets listed in shooting order showing the names of the actors, props, crew, effects, and so on, down one side, and something to indicate exactly when they will be needed. This list should be distributed and made available to all the cast and crew at the beginning of the shoot. Of course, the best-laid plans can go wrong, whether through illness, weather, equipment failure, or any other circumstance. In those cases, you have to decide whether to reschedule or to make the most of what you have.

The shot list should be a guide to what you think you can realistically shoot in the day. If you can squeeze in more, so much the better; if it's less, then you are in trouble, as the shortfall will affect the other shooting days. This tends to be a problem with larger productions where the sheer number of people makes things move slowly, and causes budgets to inflate more quickly. When this happens, an amended schedule has to be produced and distributed.

For your first few films, you should definitely make a list of all the shots you need, and organize them into a practical order in relation to locations and cast and crew availability. However, if possible, don't give yourself a time limit, because until you have some experience you won't be able to know how long each shot or setup will take. Take your time but don't waste time, either. As you finish each setup or shot, write down how long it took so you will soon be able to plan a fairly accurate schedule.

CALL SHEET

[Production title] / [Director's name] Producer: [Name] / [Telephone] Line Producer: [Name] / [Telephone] 1st Assistant Director: [Name] / [Telephone] 2nd Assistant Director: [Name] / [Telephone] 3rd Assistant Director: [Name] / [Telephone]	Date: [mm/dd/yyyy] Start time: [hh:mm] Wrap time: [hh:mm]

Location information
[include address, car/public transport directions]

Scene #	Script page	Int/Ext	Description	Day/Night	Story day	Eighths (pages)	Cast

Actor #	Actor name	Character name	Pick-up time	On set to rehearse	Makeup/ Costume	Turnover	

Additional information
(Include details of any special effects or stunts to be done today

Advance call for next day:

Scene #	Script page	Int/Ext	Description	Day/Night	Story day	Eighths (pages)	Cast

CALL SHEET ⬆

The call sheet works in conjunction with the shooting schedule. These are distributed to the cast and crew at least the day before the shoot, if not sooner. The longer the shoot, the more chance it will change on a daily basis.

CHECK THESE OUT

www.junglesoftware.com Gorilla scheduling and production software. Demo available.

www.entertainmentpartners.com MovieMagic Scheduling software. Demo available.

www.filmmakersoftware.com A comprehensive scheduling and budgeting software for $15 (requires Microsoft Excel).

LOCATION

LOW-BUDGET, OR GUERRILLA FILMMAKING RELIES ALMOST TOTALLY ON SHOOTING ON LOCATION. BUILDING SETS AND HIRING STUDIOS COME SO FAR DOWN THE BUDGET PRIORITY LIST THAT THE TOPIC NEED NOT EVEN BE BROACHED IN THIS BOOK. OF COURSE, IF YOU ARE LUCKY ENOUGH TO GET THE USE OF A STUDIO, AND IT CAN BE DRESSED FOR NOTHING, THAT'S ANOTHER MATTER.

- ▶▶ Shooting in public spaces
- ▶▶ Insurance
- ▶▶ Interior locations

Shooting on location isn't just about saving money—you may have to pay for using that old warehouse—it's about realism. Big-budget Hollywood features tend to look at using locations from a different perspective, which does involve economics, and the ability to control the environment. The size of a feature-film crew means that the sheer cost of moving it, along with lighting and camera rigs, can outweigh the cost of building the set in a studio. Shooting on location also adds other variables, such as time constraints determined by disruption to public life, and uncontrollable factors such as natural phenomena (weather, light). All sorts of permits are required before you can shoot in public spaces and thoroughfares, and it only takes one unexpected event to send the schedule spiraling out of control. There are plenty of documented examples.

TAKING IT TO THE STREETS

Filming guerrilla-style, on the other hand, does mean you can shoot quickly and adapt easily to changes. It also means taking certain risks when shooting in public. It is often illegal to make movies in public places without permission from the authorities. The thrill of being an outlaw soon vanishes if an officious policeman confiscates your equipment.

RESTAURANT/DINER ▶▶

Many restaurant owners will be quite happy to let you shoot in their establishments for nothing, as long as it doesn't interfere with their business and you give them a credit. Most restaurants have at least one half day a week when they are closed to the public, while others are only open in the evenings so you can shoot during the day. Kitchen staff use this time to prepare ingredients, which could cause sound recording problems, or simply add the required ambience. Make sure there is enough space for your crew to work and set up lights if necessary. Mirrors on the walls can cause problems. Restore any furniture to its original position at the end of the shoot. You will have to pay for the meals that get served, and watch for continuity issues if they are being eaten.

OFFICE/STOCKBROKERS ▶▶

For a simple open plan or cubicled office, you can arrange to do your shoot over a weekend. Ambient sound can be recorded at a different time to make it sound realistic. On the other hand, shooting in a stockbrokers' office will be very difficult on a low budget. They are unlikely to let you disrupt their normal business during trading hours, and outside of that it will be difficult to achieve a level of credibility as the frenetic activity will be too hard to imitate. Showing the right data on computers out of trading hours could be difficult, although the markets are always online somewhere in the world. Note that it can be difficult to shoot computers as you get horizontal banding, although the new LCD screens don't suffer from this.

Because of the money involved in filmmaking, most major cities have agencies or departments dedicated to overseeing, coordinating, and issuing permits for film shoots. It is always worth contacting them to find out the legal requirements and costs for filming in public. They will require details of your shoot, but don't give them too much information, such as your name or the exact date or intended location, in case their stipulations and costs necessitate a more covert operation. Explain that it is a no-budget film and you want to do the right thing. If you have any students on your crew, you can try the old student project line. Naturally, if the shoot involves an action sequence with a car chase or firearms (even fake ones), it is imperative to inform the police to avoid jail or physical injury, or both—which brings up the issue of insurance (see Safety Policies, right).

INSIDE JOBS

Interior locations present a whole different set of problems, depending on whether you want to use private, civil, or civic premises. You still need to obtain permission from the owner or management of the property and fit the shoot in around their schedule, which usually means after hours. As you are relying on

goodwill, you have to accept their terms and adjust your shooting, or even the script, to suit. Often the best approach is to find as many freely available locations as you can, and develop your story around them.

During pre-production, you or the producer should visit the location and draw up a clear contractual agreement with the owners, including a detailed inventory. No matter how friendly you all are in the beginning, if something goes wrong and it starts getting nasty, you need to have yourself covered. It will also lend you an air of professionalism that may work in your favor when dealing with bureaucrats.

Whichever way you decide to work, once you have decided on the locations, draw up a list, agree dates with the owners or managers, sign any contracts, and add the locations and dates to your shooting schedule (see pages 42–43).

SAFETY POLICIES

Without entering into a debate on the moral basis of insurance, it is the case that if you are shooting a movie on location with a cast and crew you should get some public liability coverage. In these litigious times, if something were to go wrong, not having sufficient insurance could end your film career before it starts—unless you want to make a documentary on the legal and penal system. Without insurance, you will not be issued a permit.

With outdoor locations, make sure that you have decided well in advance where you want to shoot, that you have the appropriate permits, and also that you have contingency plans. The whole point of pre-production is to make the shoot go as smoothly as possible.

PUBLIC TRANSPORTATION ▶▶

A very difficult location to shoot. If you are shooting with miniDV, you can do it guerrilla-style (pretending to be a tourist) but you will have no control over the environment (such as public staring into the camera or heckling) or the continuity. Off-peak times will be easier, but it does depend whether your film needs a crowd or an empty car. The noise and movement will be problematic for both sound and camera, as will obtaining decent lighting. If you do seek permission from the operators, they will usually restrict you to off-peak times but may let you use a car to yourself, which you can fill up with extras. Doing it legally will probably cost you, but you may obtain access to the station as well. Just be very precise about your intentions.

SNOW-COVERED MOUNTAINS ▶▶

Depending on the location, you may not need to get official permission to shoot. Your biggest problem is going to be the environment. You have to ensure that there is some snow and that it is the "right type." Once snow has been walked on, it is almost impossible to restore it to a pristine condition. Reflection is going to cause havoc with exposure. The cold will affect your cast, crew, and also your equipment, as both humans and machines will refuse to work below a certain temperature. Special covers will keep cameras and batteries at working temperatures, but rapid changes between heat and cold will cause problems of condensation. A power supply is very unlikely, unless you are carrying a generator. Your working days will be very short, which your crew will appreciate.

PRODUCTION DESIGN

WHEN YOU WRITE A SCRIPT OR READ SOMEONE ELSE'S THAT YOU WANT TO DIRECT, YOU MUST HAVE A VERY CLEAR IDEA OF WHAT THE MOVIE IS GOING TO LOOK LIKE. IF YOU ARE THE WRITER, YOU MAY ALREADY HAVE SPECIFIC PLACES IN MIND, OR THEY MAY JUST BE CONCEPTS BASED ON PLACES YOU'VE SEEN. IF YOU HAVEN'T CHOSEN ANYWHERE, YOU MAY WANT TO ENLIST THE HELP OF A PRODUCTION DESIGNER.

» The overall "look"

» Dressing a scene

» Show, not tell

LOCATION, LOCATION, LOCATION ⩢

If you can't find a suitable location through your friends or family, you can try a professional location finder—but they cost. Alternatively, change your script to use a location you can get for nothing.

WHAT DOES THE PRODUCTION DESIGNER DO?

The role of the production designer is to create the overall look of everything that appears in front of the cameras, from sets and props to costumes and even hairstyles. If you have the luxury of a studio shoot, the production designer, in consultation with the director, will devise the sets, and oversee their construction and the buying or renting of props. For the lo-no budget movie, you are more likely to be shooting in borrowed locations, and in borrowed time if they are public property, so that sort of attention to detail is not always possible.

SCENE STEALING

If you are lucky enough to have a more flexible use of a location, you may need to "dress" it. This usually involves emptying the room and decorating it in a fashion that suits a character or the film. The production designer, along with a location manager, takes care of this. Sometimes this "dressing" goes beyond just changing the furniture to repainting the walls. This has to be negotiated and agreed with the property owner, and usually entails restoring the location to its original color after the shoot—unless you can convince them how wonderful your taste in interior decorating is.

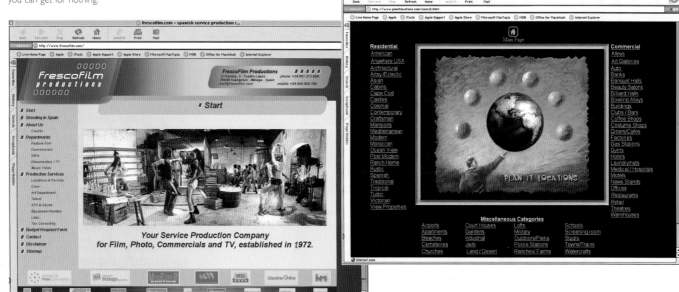

On low-budget movies these sorts of cosmetic changes will add up to wasted time and money. Making the most of what you have is a very practical approach. A bit of uncluttering can help to remove unwanted distractions from the background, but anything else would be superfluous. Ideally, you don't want the setting to dominate the scene, or steal it from the actors, so it should be kept as natural as possible.

The type of film you are making will dictate your approach to production design. If the movie has lots of fast-moving action or fight scenes, the sets will have to be designed to accommodate the fight choreography, or vice versa. For exteriors, the production designer will make suggestions for locations, but with no budget you will not always be able to shoot in the place you want. Even working guerrilla-style, action sequences are likely to attract unwanted attention, usually from the police.

If the movie has lots of dialogue, with the focus on the actors, backgrounds may not be very important and shouldn't impose. On the other hand, because you have only a very limited time to develop a character's personality, a lot can be conveyed through the production design. Simple things like the pictures on the wall, the style of furniture, and general cleanliness (or lack of it) are all devices for conveying personality traits to the audience. One of the edicts of good writing and storytelling is "to show, not tell," and this is even more important, and easier, in visual media. Take advantage of it.

Good production design should be invisible, just as the cinematography and sound should be, which means you shouldn't notice it. If you hear people talking about how great the picture looked, and nothing else, then you know your film didn't work. Everything has to be balanced so that they say, "What a great movie." It should look fantastic, but not at the expense of the story.

LIVING LARGE ▲
Large, specially constructed sets like this one are the preserve of large budgets, but location shoots still need the same attention to detail that purpose-built sets require.

COMPUTER GENERATED ▲
Building computer models of sets helps with construction, lighting, and camera movements. Today, whole sets are built in the computer and live actors are added to them (for example, *Sin City*, *Sky Captain*, *Star Wars*).

PLAN ▶▶
If you are lucky enough to have the use of a studio, planning is essential to make sure your sets fit into the space. Rooms will be made up of movable flat panels to facilitate the cameras.

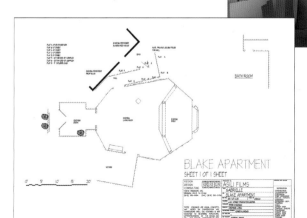

BLAKE APARTMENT
SHEET 1 OF 1 SHEET

COSTUME AND MAKEUP

ONCE YOU'VE DRESSED THE SET, YOU HAVE TO DRESS THE ACTORS.

THE MORE AMBITIOUS YOUR PROJECT, THE MORE COMPLEX IT BECOMES FOR THE WARDROBE DEPARTMENT.

▶▶ Low-budget costumes and makeup

▶▶ Costuming logistics

▶▶ Production design

SPECIAL EFFECTS ⯯
Special effects makeup requires hours of application. For the short film *Annabel*, the actress was made up as an accident victim. Latex wounds were created for the leg and stomach.

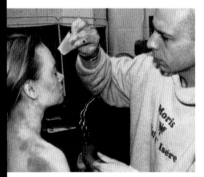

PERIOD COSTUMES ▶▶
Local amateur theater groups may have elaborate costumes they will lend you, or rent at favorable rates, especially if you can offer your talents in exchange.

Gritty urban drama won't require much more than the clothes the actors themselves own, or a quick visit to the local thrift store. Once you start moving into genre movies, you will need to enlist the assistance of someone who is handy with a sewing machine, or the telephone number of your local costume rental store or amateur dramatic group.

For your first film, it's unlikely you are going to attempt a period costume drama. If you are, good luck. Contemporary drama is the most popular genre, followed by horror and sci-fi. The beauty of the last two is that they can be produced without elaborate costumes and makeup. It is often overlooked that science fiction is a story with a scientific base, and it does not have to involve futuristic space travel.

Horror is about scaring people, and it does not need monsters; in fact, what you can't see is usually more frightening than any latex mask.

MAKEUP
Even without going into special effects, you are going to need someone on your team to apply basic makeup. This is usually no more than face powder, to take the shine off skin under lights. They must also ensure that hairstyles remain consistent throughout scenes. Most women have experience applying their own makeup and should have no problem adapting their skill to making up others. If you want someone more skilled or professional, but don't have the budget, try using your charms, and the mystique of movies, to approach the people who work as demonstrators at the cosmetic counters in department stores. Better still, if you are male, send your girlfriend or sister for a free makeover and get them to drop the subject into the conversation.

Another potential source of labor is colleges. Working with students has its advantages and disadvantages. They may be happy to get credits

CHEAP AND CHEERFUL ◀◀
Thrift and cheap fashion stores are a great source of clothes for costumes, especially if you are after the "trashy" look.

for their audition tapes, but they are also an obvious choice for every low-budget and student filmmaker, so they can be in demand. Alternatively, approach an amateur dramatics association. These are a great resource for budding filmmakers. Although stage makeup is more exaggerated than that for film, the principle is the same. These associations can also be a good place to find elaborate costumes.

ALL DRESSED UP

Although every production is different, the basic rules and requirements remain the same. If your shoot is going to last more than one day, you will need a person to run your wardrobe. Even if your actors are supplying their own costumes, you need someone to coordinate the logistics. When a shoot lasts longer than a day, it is especially important that actors do not wear their costumes to the shoot—they must be left with the wardrobe person. Allowing actors to leave the shoot in their costumes is courting disaster, as the clothes risk being dirtied or, worse, being left at

home. Polaroids were a standard tool of costume departments, used to keep a record of who wore what and how, but digital still cameras are a lot more convenient, economical, and efficient, especially if used with a laptop computer.

Apart from the organizational aspect, the wardrobe person/department has to work in conjunction with the production designer. Not only do the costumes have to fit the characters, but the choice of colors and patterns can influence the look and meaning of the finished movie. For example, in Warren Beatty's *Dick Tracy* the costumes used bold, flat colors to enhance the overall "comic book" look of the film. They are subtle details that may go unnoticed but do make a difference, just as giving a character a particular color to wear can add symbolic meaning.

Getting the wardrobe and makeup organized before the shoot, even if it's a guerrilla-style movie, will make everything run that much more smoothly on the day of filming.

PROFESSIONAL MAKEUP ▲
Makeup artists carry huge amounts of supplies to cater to most situations. This can range from simply taking the shine off the skin (essential, especially under direct light) to aging someone, or making them look unhealthy. More complex work usually requires giving the artist advance warning.

GENRES

After you cast your favorite actors, transform them with makeup into the exact characters you envisioned when you wrote your script. Get a professional makeup person on board, if at all possible.

CLASSIC MAKEUP

Use shading and highlighting to improve the face. Fluid foundations work well for film and television. Shade the cheekbone hollows if they need more structure.

FANTASY

Prosthetics are useful when creating fantasy figures. This false nose adds just the right touch. Spirit gum is used to attach the fake eyebrows and chin whiskers. Dark foundation and a stippling of brownish-red will help to weather the face.

ACCIDENT

It isn't difficult to create a black or damaged eye that looks totally genuine. A road accident victim is likely to have one, if not both, eyes bruised or somehow affected by the trauma of the collision.

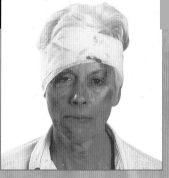

HISTORICAL

The simple application of side whiskers transforms this actor into a gentleman who might easily have lived in the Victorian period. Strengthen natural age lines with dark brown pencil.

THE SHOOT

After all the preparation, and with the schedule planned out, you will be eager to get on with what most people would consider to be real filmmaking—the shoot. It is certainly the most intense part of the process and usually the shortest. If you have done all your pre-production correctly, that is how it should be.

You will now have other people involved in order to divide the workload, but if there is payment involved, you have a vested interest in getting it done quickly. Even if the cast and crew are working for free, there is a limit to how much of their time you can take up, unless they are as committed to the project as you are.

For your first directorial shoots, you can surround yourself with people who know what they are doing and learn from their expertise. This can be a rather daunting experience, as you will have to face the fact that you know nothing when you are barraged with questions about what to do next or how you want it done. Alternatively, you can try to do everything yourself, and learn from your mistakes. Both approaches have their advantages and disadvantages, and your choice will be dictated by your personality and circumstances.

This section of the book covers some of the theory of practical filmmaking, as well as providing advice on making the most of what you have to produce the best results. Of course, the only way to get results is to go out and do it, which is why theory is kept to a minimum.

LIGHTING

THE DIRECTOR OF PHOTOGRAPHY (DoP), OR CINEMATOGRAPHER, HAS TWO VERY SPECIFIC FUNCTIONS TO FILL ON A SHOOT. THE FIRST AND MOST OBVIOUS IS OPERATING, OR AT LEAST DIRECTING, THE CAMERA. THE SECOND IS LIGHTING THE SHOTS, BECAUSE WITHOUT LIGHT, ONE WOULD NOT BE ABLE TO FILM.

- ▸▸ Using natural light
- ▸▸ Affordable artificial light
- ▸▸ Lighting design

A badly lit scene is going to ruin your movie as much as bad acting or poor sound. The way a scene is lit will change its mood and your audience's perception of what you are trying to express. For the low-budget filmmaker, having a truckload of lights is out of the question, so how do you get the best possible lighting without spending a fortune?

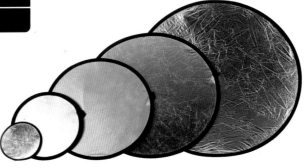

COLOR TEMPERATURE ❧

Film and video are affected by color temperature. The chart is divided into kelvins (sometimes called degrees kelvin), and shows an approximation of how they look. To obtain accurate color with film, you compensate by using filters or the appropriate stock, or in the case of video by adjusting the white balance. The chart clarifies why photos shot indoors on daylight film (5,500 k) appear orange, and sunsets always look so much more vibrant.

REFLECTOR RANGE ▸▸
Portable reflectors are indispensable, both in the studio and on location. They come in a variety of sizes and colors, and fold down into small carry bags.

NATURAL LIGHT

The simplest way is to use existing light, the light that is around you. Natural daylight is the best, although shooting in the noonday sun is going to give very contrasting images. This can be overcome either by diffusing the sunlight through thin cloth shades or by using filler lights to remove hard shadows.

Alternatively, you can use reflectors, which are simply large reflective surfaces that bounce a source light on to your actors to soften shadows. Foldable reflectors can be bought from professional photography suppliers, or you can make your own reflector with a thin sheet of polystyrene foam or Foamcore board and some kitchen foil. Simply glue

▸▸▸▸▸ SEE ALSO
Pages 56–57 *Shooting Basics*

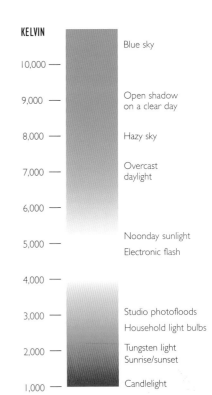

KELVIN

10,000 —	Blue sky
9,000 —	Open shadow on a clear day
8,000 —	Hazy sky
7,000 —	Overcast daylight
6,000 —	
5,000 —	Noonday sunlight Electronic flash
4,000 —	
3,000 —	Studio photofloods Household light bulbs
2,000 —	Tungsten light Sunrise/sunset
1,000 —	Candlelight

BACKLIGHT ◀◀

Strong backlight is very difficult to work with and needs very careful calculation of the exposure, according to the effect you want to convey. In this scene from Stanley Kubrick's *A Clockwork Orange*, the unnaturally strong backlighting was used here to create the sense of a foreboding menace, with the actors being left in silhouette. If the exposure reading was taken from the faces, the surrounding scene would have been burned out, creating this "angels arriving" effect.

DAYLIGHT ▶▶

Light cloud cover will give very even light without much contrast, which is useful for creating an atmospheric mood. Unfortunately it is not possible to have any control over natural light.

INTERIOR SETS ◀◀

By setting the exposure for the lighting on the left of this scene, from David Fincher's *Seven*, the very strong light source becomes overexposed, giving more contrast to the shot. The use of a smoke machine helps create defined beams from the flashlights.

the foil onto one side of the sheet and leave the other side white. As they are a little more cumbersome to transport than the reflectors you can buy, if you plan to do lots of outdoor shooting involving traveling, you should definitely invest in the manufactured, foldable ones.

Natural light is also wonderful for daytime interiors. Unfortunately, it does change as the day progresses, and you will need to plan your shoot carefully to take full advantage of it. Make use of reflectors here as well.

ARTIFICIAL LIGHT

Using artificial light involves spending money. How much depends on the look you want or the amount of improvisation you are prepared to do. The majority of affordable lighting is tungsten, which has a lower color temperature than daylight (see chart). If you are shooting on film, you will have to use a tungsten-balanced stock. Daylight film will have a warm, orange cast under tungsten. With videotape you can simply change your camera's white balance to the tungsten preset. Avoid using auto white balance or trying to do it manually. If you mix light sources, it will create unnatural colors, as the daylight will get a blue cast using a tungsten-balanced medium. Pale orange cel over the windows should resolve the problem.

The cheapest form of artificial light is the high-wattage practical light bulb or photoflood available from photographic equipment suppliers. These will fit

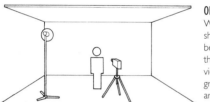

ONE LIGHT
When using one light, the shadows on the wall become more noticeable as the angle between camera view and light direction grows. Normally shadows are avoided, but they can be used to great effect.

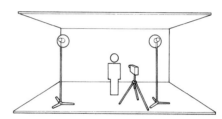

TWO LIGHTS
When the main, or key, light is placed at 45° to the camera view, and the second, or "fill," light is placed close to the camera with a direction close to its viewpoint, extremes of light and darkness are avoided.

into most domestic light sockets and remain hidden. Other solutions are the tungsten or halogen floodlights used on construction sites. These give off a lot of light and heat that is difficult to control and work with, but they are inexpensive.

For low-budget filmmakers needing a decent artificial light source, redheads are the most popular choice. These are available in a package with stands and barn doors, and will cost you around $1,000 for three lights. They also give off a lot of heat.

Photographic fluorescent tubes provide an alternative. These are balanced for either tungsten or daylight. (Standard domestic tubes give off a green light so they are not suitable.) Professional lighting rigs are available, but if you are handy, and know an electrician, you can make your own. Fluorescents are much cooler than standard tungsten and use a lot less electricity, but can take up more space, which may not be available in a small location.

Remember, when designing your lighting it is important to make it look realistic and natural, unless you are deliberately trying to create an atmospheric mood or special effect. If you are shooting on DV you must ensure you don't over-light, which causes the whites to burn out, or under-light, which results in grainy images with lots of artifacts. Get your lighting right and your movie will definitely look a lot more professional than the average low-budget DV offering.

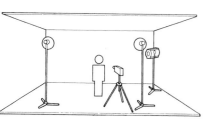

THREE LIGHTS
The addition of a third light means that the background can be illuminated. Any shadows on the walls can be eliminated and the background given the best exposure level. Take care that other parts of the scene are not affected.

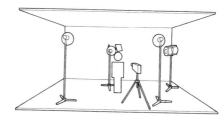

FOUR LIGHTS
The fourth light is normally a backlight, which can add a halo glow to the subject, and depth and dimension to a scene. There is a risk of flare, even when, as is usually the case, the light is highly placed.

SHOOTING BASICS

ONCE YOU HAVE SORTED OUT THE LIGHTING, YOU ARE READY TO START SHOOTING. OR ARE YOU? THE SHOOT IS THE MOST CRUCIAL PART OF THE PRODUCTION CYCLE, BECAUSE WHATEVER HAPPENS AT THIS STAGE WILL DETERMINE THE OUTCOME OF YOUR MOVIE.

▶▶ Film stock

▶▶ Achieving the film "look" using video

STANDARD GAUGES ▶▶
The three main sizes of film used for cinematography: 35mm, 16mm, and Super 8 (shown actual size). The 35mm is shown at its standard 4:3 ratio, as is the 16mm. Super 16 has only one set of sprockets to allow the wider frame ratio, which means it cannot accept a soundtrack, and has to be blown up to 35mm for viewing.

There are lots of things you can do in post-production to recover from mistakes but it is far better to avoid them in the first place, and this can be done simply by knowing your equipment. If you are not familiar with the functions and limitations of your camera, you are courting disaster.

You should have decided a long time back which medium you are going to shoot on—video or film—and which format. If you are shooting on film, there are many things to consider beyond its gauge (Super 8, 16mm, Super 16). You have to pick a stock to match not only the shooting environment but also the mood of the movie: black and white or color, then positive or negative, and finally the film's speed. Color or black and white will be the director's decision, while the director of photography will make the others. Most films are shot on negative stock as it offers greater exposure latitude and is better suited to duplication. The original negative is preserved for making the final cut, with work prints used for editing, although it is more common to get it digitized for editing (telecine). With Super 8, positive stock is better if it is going to be cut by hand, as the size of the film does not really lend itself to duplication or enlargement. When negative stock is used, it has to be telecined for editing on digital systems, for the same reason.

The speed of the film determines its sensitivity to light, so a higher number (e.g., ISO 400) will work better in low light, but will have more "grain," or larger particles of silver. The type of lighting also has to be factored into the equation for selecting the film. Daylight requires daylight-balanced film, and artificial light needs tungsten film. It is possible to employ the same film under different lighting conditions, providing filters are used on the lens or gels over the light sources. This will reduce the amount of light reaching the film, affecting the exposure, making it yet another thing to consider.

With digital video there is no need to calculate all the permutations and combinations, as the variables will be dictated by the capabilities of your camera, including whether you shoot in widescreen or not (see pages 62–63).

The holy grail of video is getting it to look like film. While the obvious solution is simply to use film, there are techniques that can alter the appearance of video to give it that elusive "film look." A basic step to take is to treat your video shoot as though you were shooting film. This means proper lighting and carefully (manually) controlled exposure settings. These will

35mm   16mm   Super 8

FOCAL LENGTH ▶▶
Camera lenses come in different focal lengths for different uses. A wide-angle lens will show a lot more foreground, but will make the background seem farther away, whereas a telephoto will bring distant objects closer, including the background, giving a compressed feeling.

WIDE-ANGLE LENS ▲   STANDARD LENS ▲   TELEPHOTO LENS ▲

ADJUSTING FOCUS ▶▶
The different required focus points are marked on a white ring so that the focus puller can make the necessary adjustments without having to look through the lens. It is a skilled job that requires a lot of practice.

MEASURE FOR MEASURE ▶▶
To ensure accurate focus, especially with film cameras, a tape measure is used and the distance set on the lens focus ring. This is more reliable than focusing visually, and allows a focus puller to control it while the camera operator concentrates on the image.

improve the look of your shoot no matter which medium you are using.

But to achieve that film look you should also use something known as "Progressive Scan," which is available on some top-end DV cameras. Here comes the science. Most video cameras capture interlaced images, which simply means that two alternating images are captured and joined to create a single image. Progressive Scan captures a single image, similar to the way film is exposed one frame at a time. Further to emulate film, 24 frames are captured per second. This is known as 24P video. In countries that use the NTSC video standard, which runs at 30fps (frames per second), 24P makes a significant difference. PAL, the other major video format, runs at 25fps, and cameras in PAL countries are generally 25P.

Even if you intend to transfer to film, shoot at 25fps and sort out the transfer in post-production. In PAL countries it is advisable to shoot film at 25fps (if your camera allows), rather than the standard 24fps, as it will make the telecine/editing process much easier. More about video formats and film-look is covered in the post-production section (see pages 100–101), but if you want to achieve the look of film with video, you have to use Progressive Scan.

YOU WILL NEED
Batteries (fully charged)

Camera

Changing bag for loading film

Film/tapes

Power supply and/or battery charger

Lenses (if your camera takes changeable ones)

Tape measure

Lens hoods and "flags"

Tripod and other supports

Gaffer tape

Reflectors

Slate/clapperboard

Notebooks, pens

UNUSUAL POINT OF VIEW ▶▶

The director places the camera in the back of the vehicle. This provides an unusual point of view, which can be used to strengthen the plot as the audience becomes privy to something the other character in the scene is unaware of.

Cinematography is a technical pursuit. It has its creative side, but most importantly it is about getting the shots, and making sure they are properly exposed, correctly color-balanced, and in focus. It is also the responsibility of the director to ensure that enough coverage is shot. This will be done in consultation with the DoP who, on a low-budget film, could also be the director.

Coverage means getting a variety of shots for each scene. These can be: an establishing shot that is a wide-angle of the whole scene; medium shots, showing the main protagonists; and close-ups of each person talking—often done as over-the shoulder-shots (see page 61 for the problem of "crossing the line"). The other shots needed are cutaways—close-ups of hands, panoramas, POV shots out of windows. These can directly relate to the immediate action, adding to dramatic detail or providing important story information, or may simply be a way to break up the monotony of talking heads.

On feature films, the B unit, a separate crew that works independently, often after the main shooting is done, handles this. On low-budget films (or videos), the luxury of a separate B unit is out of reach, but for a small outlay (the price of a camera), you can increase your coverage while minimizing shooting time. A two-camera shoot can really save you a lot of time, give you added editing options, and the security of two tapes of each setup.

Positioning the cameras is important, not only to ensure that they don't appear in the frame, but also to get the best possible angles. You may decide to keep one of the cameras static on a tripod (locked

AMENDED SHOT LIST ▼

During the shoot, shots are altered, joined, or added. Marking changes on the original shot list serves as a backup to the shot log and will help the editor. Get the AD or continuity person to write the changes.

Ticking off the shots helps the AD keep track of what has been done.

A different angle was added to the original storyboard idea.

It was decided it would be easier and more natural for the actor to do the action in one take, moving the camera with the Steadicam.

This was an afterthought and was shot during a logical pause in the shoot.

These inserts were decided at the time. Shot 9 was not set up, but actually existed on the set.

It was decided that a greater variety of shots were needed for the edit. All of these had to be done before the face was shaved as there was no chance of reshooting after that.

Crisis Shot list Day 1

Scene 1 Bedroom

1. ECU: Sleeping man's face, girl's hand lifting man's eyelid. Wide Angle lens
2. CU: Girl's face. Strong backlight. WA.
3. MCU: pulls back to MS over the shoulder shot of man in bed.
4. MS: Overhead of man in be next to sleeping wife, as bed cover moves down bed. Pulls back to MLS revealing children pulling covers. *Add tracking shot that follows the bedcover, shot beside*   *5 & 7 combined into 1 steadicam shot*
5. MC: Man sitting in bed looking at wife.
6. CU: Man's POV of sleeping wife.
7. MLS: Man climbs out of bed, we follow him as he kisses her and pulls covers back over her.
15. CU of man kissing wife to be inserted at edit.

Scene 2 Kitchen
7. MS: Man preparing breakfast for children *cereal pouring into bowls.*
8. CU insert shot of photo of man's guru surrounded by *bottles of vitamins and stress supplements*
9. CU insert shot of

Scene 3 Dining room
10. MLS: Man places cereal on table and we follow him into the bathroom stopping at closing door.
11. MCU of children eating

Scene 4 Bathroom
12. CU: Over shoulder shot of man looking in mirror.
13. BCU: Mirror's POV of man studying face, nose, eyes, tongue, hairline, lathering up and shaving. Shot several times. *Over shoulder shots w/ mirror added.*
14. MCU: Over shoulder of man opening cabinet and studying available after shave lotions then applying one to face.
15. CU of man kissing wife in bedroom (scene 1)

INSERT ▶▶

Insert shots, such as close-ups of hands, here checking a watch, help with the storytelling and act as transitions between shots in editing.

SHOT LOG ⤓

The assistant camera person, or the camera person on a small crew, marks down all the details of each shot as it is taken so the editor knows exactly what he or she has to work with.

The slate number is matched to the number on the shot list.

Good shots are indicated so the editor knows to ignore the ones not marked.

This was shot out of sequence because it was easier for continuity to keep the girl in the one place while the camera was behind her. They were also waiting for the sun to shine through the window for the backlighting.

A variation on the original listed shot.

This was three takes but the camera was kept running, so it was only slated once.

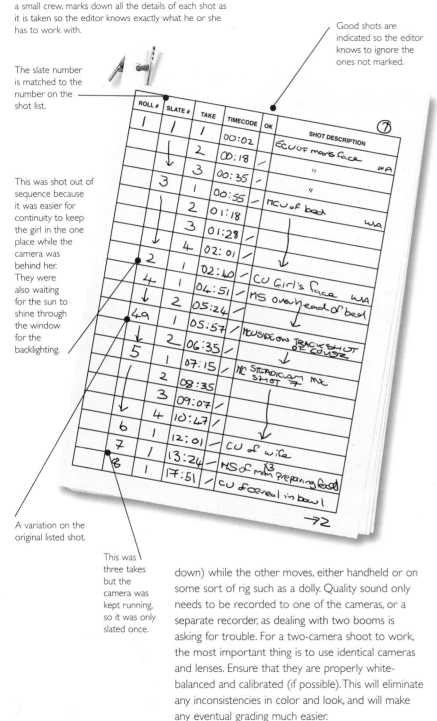

ROLL #	SLATE #	TAKE	TIMECODE	OK	SHOT DESCRIPTION
1	1	1	00:02		
		2	00:18	/	ECU of man's face WA
		3	00:35	/	"
	3	1	00:55		"
		2	01:18	/	MCU of bed WA
		3	01:28	/	
		4	02:01	/	
2		1	02:40	/	CU Girl's face WA
	4	1	04:51	/	MS overhead of bed
		2	05:24	/	
4a		1	05:57	/	MCU dolly TRACKING SHOT of couple
		2	06:35	/	
5		1	07:15	/	MC STEADICAM MX SHOT 7
		2	08:35		
		3	09:07	/	
		4	10:47	/	
6		1	12:01	/	CU of wife
7		1	13:24	/	MS of man preparing food
8		1	17:51		cu of cereal in bowl

→72

down) while the other moves, either handheld or on some sort of rig such as a dolly. Quality sound only needs to be recorded to one of the cameras, or a separate recorder, as dealing with two booms is asking for trouble. For a two-camera shoot to work, the most important thing is to use identical cameras and lenses. Ensure that they are properly white-balanced and calibrated (if possible). This will eliminate any inconsistencies in color and look, and will make any eventual grading much easier.

SHOT LIST

The cinematographer/camera person needs two lists. The first is a list of shots to be done on the day. This is usually drawn up during pre-production, and/or the night before, with the director, the producer, and the DoP. The second, which is more important, is a list of every shot taken. This is invaluable for editing.

For video you will need to create a simple sheet that lists: movie title; shooting date; roll (or tape) number; slate number; take; timecode; shot description; and a tick box. You can add other data, such as lighting source and exposure settings, but these are not vital and will depend on whether you can actually adjust them on the camera. If you are shooting film, you must have all that data for the lab.

Once you have created the sheet, it must be filled out before every shot. The roll or tape number—obviously starting at 1 (or 001 if you prefer)—is written on the tape and also on its storage case. How they are coded is entirely up to you, as long as you know in which order they are shot and the film's title.

The slate number is the same as the setup or shot number from the shooting schedule. The take number is the number of times each set-up is shot. The timecode is the running time of the tape shown as HH:MM:SS:FF (hours : minutes : seconds : frames) and is recorded onto a separate track on the tape that does not show up when played back, unless you want it to. This is different from the date and time, which many consumer cameras embed into the scene. Most decent miniDV cameras will record timecode, with pro cameras having manual adjust as well, so that each tape can be consecutively registered. Putting this on the sheet before each shot makes it easier to find when transferring to a computer for editing.

The shot description should be basic—start with Int or Ext, and include shot type (LS, MS, CU, etc.). The tick box allows you to indicate if the take was usable. The information on the sheet should match what you write on the clapperboard (see page 17).

Although this seems over-meticulous and time-consuming, it will eventually save you a lot of time. These are some of the important basics of cinematography. There are more details of other aspects on the following pages.

COMPOSITION

COMPOSITION—AN ARTISTIC ASPECT OF FILMMAKING THAT IS HARD TO QUANTIFY—IS THE WAY THE ELEMENTS ARE PLACED WITHIN YOUR FRAME, AND THEIR POSITIONING AND RELATIONSHIP TO ONE ANOTHER. A LOT OF IT IS SUBJECTIVE AND WILL OFTEN OCCUR INTUITIVELY AND/OR ACCIDENTALLY.

- ▸▸ Division of thirds
- ▸▸ Camera lens & position
- ▸▸ Other composition rules

OVER THE SHOULDER ▸▸
Shooting over the shoulder shots like this, you have to be very careful of not crossing the line when reversing the shot.

CAMERA A
The establishing shot of the sequence, taken with camera A. This can be over the shoulder, as shown, or simply with the facing character.

CAMERA B
The opposing shot, from camera B, either over the shoulder or solo character, when edited gives the impression the two characters are facing each other as they appear on opposite sides of the screen.

CAMERA C
Although it would seem logical to shoot with camera C, over the same shoulder of the two characters, by doing this and crossing the line, it would disorient the viewer to have both characters appear on the same side of the screen during the intercuts.

Studying still images, such as paintings and photographs, is one of the best ways to learn about composition. Of course, films have the added dimension of movement, which means that your composition is in a constant state of flux, whereas photographs capture a single moment.

While there are some basic "rules" of composition that are worth following, intuition plays a large part, as do "luck" and "accidents" (what photographer Henri Cartier-Bresson called "the decisive moment"), although the last two are less likely to occur in the controlled environment of a film set.

THIRD DIVISIONS
One of the principal guides for composition is the division of thirds. Divide your screen horizontally and vertically into three, and then place the actors, objects, or scenery into the nine subdivisions. If you weren't already aware of this, the next time you watch a film look at how the shots are framed and you will notice that the actors are usually placed at the edge of the screen. As most movies are shot in widescreen, this presents problems when they are transferred to the "small screen" ratio of 4:3 using the "pan and scan" process, unless the letterbox format is used, which will tend to cut off one of the actors.

Even if you are shooting in 4:3 format, you can still divide your screen into thirds, but the composition changes slightly and your actors will have to work much closer together. Placing an actor's face right in the center of the screen, with lots of space above it and around it, is a mistake often made by first-time filmmakers, but that does not mean it cannot be used

to achieve a particular effect. It all depends on execution and intent.

FOCUS GROUPS
Your composition will also be dictated by your choice of camera lens, position, and the mood or effect you want to achieve. For example, shooting an actor from a low position gives that person an air of authority, while shooting from above diminishes his or her power. By altering the camera position relative to the character as the story progresses, you can subtly enforce changes in his or her role. A similar effect can be achieved by choosing a particular lens for a certain character's personality. A long lens will tend to isolate the actor from the background, which goes out of focus. This can be used both for people who are too self-important and for loners who feel they can't fit in. Equally, a wide-angle lens can be used to evoke a feeling of loneliness, as the character is not being differentiated from his or her surroundings.

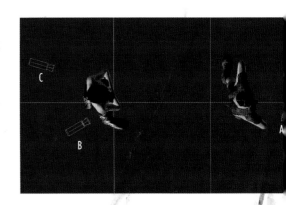

DIVISION OF THIRDS ◀◀

Dividing your frame into thirds vertically and horizontally is a great aid to composition. You don't need to put the lines on the viewfinder, as approximation is fine.

The gray horizontal lines show the division for the widescreen (16:9) version.

Notice how the character's facial features remain within the central division in both formats.

The red horizontal lines show the division for the Academy (4:3) screen version.

The gray bands top and bottom show how a letterbox widescreen would look when shot on a 4:3 camera. Because the composition allows for both versions, it is more acceptable to cut off the tops of the heads than having to reduce the sides, leaving a large chasm on the screen.

CROSSING THE LINE

Almost as complicated as the offside rule in soccer, the 180° rule, or "crossing the line," is one of the fundamentals that has to be understood in order to avoid disorienting the viewer. When filming two people facing each other, you have to keep the camera on the same side of an imaginary line drawn through the middle of them. Even though it would seem logical to film both of them over the same shoulder, it does not work (see diagram and pictures below). And just like the offside rule, even professionals can get it wrong.

EYE LINE

A bad eye line is a much easier mistake to make than crossing the line. The eye line is where the actor looks when he or she is being filmed in a single shot. Looking directly into the camera is generally frowned upon, unless it is a talking-to-the-audience shot. Even for point-of-view shots, it is better if the actor can look away slightly. Most people never make real eye-to-eye contact in conversation but focus on another part of the face—the mouth or the eyebrows. Having another actor behind the camera will often help with this.

CHECK THESE OUT

Amélie (Dir. Jean-Pierre Jeunet) Every shot is perfectly composed yet never superfluous to the story.

Paintings of Edward Hopper Striking and deceptively simple compositions that tell enigmatic stories.

Photographs of Henri Cartier-Bresson The master of black and white photojournalism who managed to capture the decisive moment, when action and composition were in harmony.

CAMERA A   CAMERA B   CAMERA C

FRAMING

NOW THAT YOU HAVE FAMILIARIZED YOURSELF WITH YOUR CAMERA, YOU ARE READY TO SHOOT, BUT WHICH FORMAT IS THE BEST? IN THIS CASE, FORMAT REFERS TO THE SHAPE OR RATIO OF THE MEDIUM, WHICH IS RATHER DICTATED BY THE TYPE OF CAMERA YOU ARE USING.

When it comes to shooting digital video there are different frame sizes and resolutions, depending on the cameras format and CCDs. This shows all the different varieties from HDV to miniDV. It does not differentiate between interlaced and progressive scan.

HDV1080I ⬆
The latest HDV cameras offer high-resolution images in a native 16:9 widescreen format. For even reasonably serious moviemakers this is the format to use. (1920 × 1080 pixels)

▶ Academy or widescreen?

▶ Faking widescreen

▶ The "safe area"

The two principal formats are Academy (4:3) and widescreen (16:9). The Academy (as in the Awards) ratio is derived from a single frame of 35mm film. Standard televisions, however, are 4:3, as are computer monitors and the default settings on most video cameras.

Widescreen is the format of the latest televisions and has been adopted for HDTV (high definition television). If you are serious about getting your work broadcast, this is the format you should be shooting in. HD cameras and most top-of-the-range professional DV cameras, and an increasing number of serious amateur cameras, will shoot in this format naturally, without resorting to digital trickery that can degrade picture quality. The technique, known as anamorphic compression, achieves the effect by compressing the width of the image in the camera, and decompressing it when played back on a widescreen television.

FAKING IT

Alternatively, an anamorphic lens can be placed in front of the main lens to compress the image. With film, another lens is placed on the projector to unsquash the image. This is how Cinemascope films are made, though they use the much wider ratio of 2.35:1. For video, it can be decompressed in post-production.

If you want to shoot widescreen on a normal video camera, without resorting to squashing the picture, you can mask it. The widescreen (1.85:1) that you see in cinemas uses this method, so why

shouldn't you? It is simply a matter of putting some gaffer tape over the monitor or your flip-out LCD screen as a guide. Some cameras have the mask built-in as an option, often called letterbox. Alternatively, instead of the very sticky gaffer tape, try using a couple of strips of color cel, from the lights, so you can see what is happening outside the masked area. If you shoot very judiciously, keeping the boom out of both frames, you can have widescreen and Academy versions in the one shoot, leaving decisions on format to the editing stage. Of course, you can add an anamorphic lens to the front of your camera, but they are not cheap and the total cost could end up as high as that of buying a 16:9 camera.

As widescreen televisions become increasingly commonplace, it makes sense to start shooting everything in this format, no matter which method you choose to achieve it. While this book is all about using affordable equipment, if you can stretch your budget to buy a proper 16:9 camera, it will serve you better and for longer. A camera like the Sony PDX10 will cost you two to three times what you pay for a consumer miniDV, but it is crammed with professional features that will make your movies look more professional. And the new consumer HDDV

720P ◀◀
A smaller HD format, still at a native 16:9. (1280 x 720 pixels)

PAL DV ANAMORPHIC ◀◀
To achieve widescreen on DV cameras, anamorphic compression is used, either with an adapter lens or through the camera's electronics. It compresses the image horizontally (as shown) to fit into the camera's 4:3 frame, which is then decompressed when viewed on a widescreen TV or a projector. (768 x 576 pixels)

NTSC DV 4:3 ◀◀
The same crop as the PAL version but at NTSC resolution. The other main difference between PAL and NTSC is the frame rate and color fidelity. (720 x 540 pixels)

PAL DV ◀◀
PAL is the television standard for countries that don't use NTSC, and offers a higher resolution that runs at 25 fps. When shooting in the 4:3 format you need to consider how the image is framed, depending on your lens. Always ensure that you shoot enough width to allow cropping for letterbox widescreen. (768 x 576 pixels)

PAL DV WIDESCREEN ◀◀
The decompressed anamorphic PAL DV. (1024 x 576 pixels)

NTSC DV ANAMORPHIC 16:9 ◀◀
The decompressed NTSC anamorphic widescreen frame. (853 x 480 pixels)

PAL DV PAN AND SCAN ◀◀
If you shoot anamorphic widescreen but need to reduce down to 4:3, you can lose some of the image, which is acceptable in this case, but with two actors facing each other it can be a disaster. (768 x 576 pixels)

cameras are offering even better options. Widescreen not only gives you a lot more area to work with, it will get you into the habit of working in a professional format and learning the best way to use the screen space.

One final thing to consider, regardless of format, is the safe area. This relates to the viewable area on a television. Many pro cameras have an option for showing this, and a field monitor will as well. Failing that, make sure you don't shoot anything vital on the very edges of the frame. Most editing software has an option to show the safe area.

The most important thing is to get on and make your movie. Don't lose valuable time agonizing over which format to use and the best way to achieve it. If shooting 4:3 is going to be easiest, then shoot 4:3; you can concentrate on 16:9 for a future film.

SAFE AREA ▶▶
Editing software has "safe area" masks. Using a professional field monitor during the shoot will help to keep you from shooting outside that area.

CAMERA MOVEMENTS

HAVING LOOKED AT THE COMPOSITION OF THE IMAGES BEING CREATED, YOU HAVE TO REMEMBER THAT YOU ARE WORKING WITH MOVING IMAGES AND THE COMPOSITION IS GOING TO CHANGE, OFTEN RAPIDLY.

- ▸▸ Choosing your moves
- ▸▸ Basic movements
- ▸▸ Handheld cameras

CAMERA MOVES SKETCHES ⯯
If you don't have access to special software, draw some rough sketches to plan your camera movements.

Long static shots, such as Omar Sharif's arrival across the desert in *Lawrence of Arabia*, are the preserve of cinema epics or art house installations.

In short films you want to keep the on-screen action flowing, a lot of which will be achieved in the editing room. Modern audiences have become used to seeing almost continuous camera movement and may become unnerved by a static camera. On the other hand, putting camera movement in just for its own sake is not always advisable. It comes down to a creative decision that you, as the director, have to make. If you are in doubt and you are working with an experienced DoP, ask his or her advice. If not, go with your instincts—you can always shoot again if it doesn't work.

Any camera movements that you intend to use should be decided at the storyboard stage.

Storyboard software, such as FrameForge, will allow you to try out different camera moves and create an animatic. Alternatively, you could use an inexpensive 3D program, like Daz|Studio or Poser, that will let you put 3D characters into a set and animate the camera. It is vital to have a clear idea of what you want to achieve before you start shooting so you can have all the right equipment on the set. Once there, you can change the shot or try other moves, but that is only possible if you have the right gear in the first place.

MAKE YOUR MOVE

The basic camera movements are pan, tilt, track, dolly, and crane. Anything else—such as aerial shots—are beyond the low-budget filmmaker, unless they have well-connected friends willing to do favors. Even cranes, tracks, and dollies come with a (rental) price tag, but inventive filmmakers can find ways of getting their shots without added expense.

Tracking and dolly shots are the most commonly used and, if well executed, they will give a professional look to your movie. Using a dolly on a track will ensure that movement is smooth, especially if done by an experienced grip, and can be accurately repeated. If you are filming in an area with smooth, flat floors, any sort of wheeled conveyance will do the job. A well-oiled wheelchair is one of the most popular low-budget solutions, as it allows the cameraman to sit comfortably and even to mount the camera on a tripod or a similar device. The weight of the wheelchair and camera operator will help to ensure that movement is smooth and even. Anything too light is hard to control precisely.

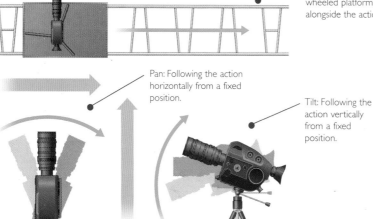

Track: Moving the camera on a wheeled platform, alongside the action.

Pan: Following the action horizontally from a fixed position.

Tilt: Following the action vertically from a fixed position.

For the guerrilla filmmaker, handheld camerawork is a staple, if not stable, method of adding movement to films. Again, weight is an issue. Most miniDV cameras are extremely light, which does mean that carrying them around all day won't wear you out. However, developing a method of carrying one while shooting so that it doesn't record every jolt of your body movement takes lots of experiment and practice. Up to a limit, the larger and heavier the camera, the more stable it is, especially if it can be mounted on the shoulder. Stabilizers and harnesses, such as Steadicams, will make movements much smoother by absorbing impact, but, like all equipment, they come with a price. It is possible to build your own stabilizer for very little money (see box), but you will still need to learn how to walk smoothly to make the most of it. Most consumer-level DV cameras come with some sort of image stabilizer, either digital or optical, that is designed to reduce visible camera shake. Switch it off!

BUILDING YOUR OWN DOLLY AND TRACK ⍦
Grip equipment is expensive to buy and rent, so ingenuity becomes an important part of low-budget filmmaking. Building your own dolly and track can be easily done with a large sheet of plywood, some angle iron, skateboard wheels, and plastic pipe.

HANDHELD ◀◀
Shoulder mounted or handheld camera shots let you get right in among the action. The weight and size of the camera will have some influence over how you execute the shot.

It will actually reduce the quality of your image during any controlled movements you make.

Cranes are used to get those shots that rise above people's heads, or swoop over a crowd. They are very complex pieces of gear, and if you need to retain complete control of your camera, to focus or to see what you are shooting, they have to be even more sophisticated. If you use a very wide-angle lens and/or autofocus, a much simpler rig can be used, or constructed, but any pan or tilt movements may have to be sacrificed, depending on the height of the jib. Even though a crane shot can look spectacular, you should ask yourself if it, or any other movement, is going to improve vastly the way your story is told.

CHECK THESE OUT
 www.homebuiltstabilizers.com
A great collection of homemade stabilizers and some instructions on how to build them

SUBSTITUTE DOLLY ▶▶
A wheelchair makes a good substitute dolly if you have a smooth surface to run it over.

CONSTRUCTING YOUR DOLLY ◀◀
Precision is needed in the construction, so get help from someone who has a workshop and the right tools.

TRACK AND DOLLY ▶▶
Lightweight, transportable track and dolly are ideal for shooting on location with DV and smaller format (16mm) film cameras, to ensure smooth, consistent shots.

Before you start planning the various camera movements and trick shots, ask yourself how they are going to improve the flow of the story. Stories are usually written in the third person ("the God view": he did this, he thought that) or the first person (I, me, mine). What narrative role is the camera playing? Whose point of view is it showing?

The narrative of your film will have some influence over your choice of camera angles and movements. For example, if you were making an urban thriller, incorporating a variety of overhead, pan, and tilt shots would add an air of credibility, imitating the ubiquitous surveillance and CCTV cameras in modern cities. You don't need any complex equipment for these shots, just a good, elevated vantage point, or a very stable ladder. You could even use the often-frowned-upon zoom to add authenticity.

ZOOM

Most DV cameras offer both optical and digital zoom. While it may be tempting to use the 300x digital zoom, don't. If you have that function, switch it off, as it gives very poor quality images. Only use the optical zoom, which will be in the range of 10x, and use that sparingly.

One of the disadvantages of using a zoom is the way it changes the background in relation to the main subject. This is caused by two factors—foreshortening and depth of field. Foreshortening is caused by the effect of a telephoto lens making the background look closer, whereas a wide-angle lens makes everything look farther away. Depth of field is the amount of the image that is in focus on either side of the main point of focus, and is influenced by the focal length and aperture of the lens. A wide-angle lens has a large depth of field that makes it ideal for handheld/Steadicam shots, as it is very forgiving, retaining focus and disguising camera shake. Long lenses, on the other hand, require very precise focusing. Even with a simple tripod-mounted pan shot, the focus has to be altered throughout the shot (this is known as "follow focus").

If you want to use a wide-to-tele zoom movement, you have to set your focus on the subject at the maximum length, then zoom it out to start the shot. Because of the depth of field, everything else will remain in focus during the zoom. Of course you will have the autofocus switched off.

The aperture controls the amount of light that passes through the lens onto the CCDs or film. Only the top range of DV cameras will allow manual control over this, although this feature exists on most film cameras (from Super 8 up). Without going into great detail of the physics involved, the smaller the

DIGITAL ZOOM ◀◀
While it is tempting to use the digital zoom to get close, the image quality will deteriorate as the camera is enlarging the optical image, causing pixelation. If you want an extreme close-up, you will have to either move (track) the camera, or use a camera that lets you change lenses.

OPTICAL ZOOM ◀
Optical zoom will give you the sharpest image at the lens's maximum length, but it may not be close enough for the shot you want.

aperture (which is the higher number, e.g., f16), the greater the depth of field.

It is because of the optical effects of zooming that dollies are used when a wide-to-close-up shot is needed. Using a fixed-length lens and moving the camera results in a much more natural feel, as the relationship to the background remains constant. Of course this type of dolly shot requires a carefully rehearsed follow focus.

WATCH THESE MOVES

Combining a dolly and zoom shot, so the head remains the same size and the background appears to be rushing toward the camera (see Goodfellas), has been done too many times and is best avoided, no matter how good you think it looks.

It is tempting to have a lot of camera moves to make your movie look "professional," which is not a good reason in itself. You will find out in the editing that all those movements don't quite flow together and your professional look has gone. It is much easier to cut between two static shots than two dolly shots, or a dolly and a cutaway.

Another problem is that too much emphasis is placed on getting the technical part of the shot right and not enough on capturing the actors' performances. Get a good variety of static shots, from different angles—using two cameras if necessary—and add movement in post-production, or imply it with clever editing. Eliminating tracking shots will also save you a lot of time and money.

If you want to have realistic movement in your films, keep your camera on a Steadicam-type rig. Everything will be more human, there will be no chance of tracks appearing in shot, and you will be able to get around locations a lot easier. It will even help overcome the potential legal problems of using a tripod in public places.

Using camera movements can add to your film's overall look; don't let them distract the viewer from the action.

SHOT TYPES ⯆

When specifying camera moves for the camera person, the type of shot can be described using short hand. For example, "MS on actor push in to CU" means start with a medium shot of the actor and track in for a close up. Below are the eight main shot sizes.

ECU: Extreme Close Up—where the detail fills the whole screen.

BCU: Big Close Up—more facial detail but still very tight.

CU: Close Up—just showing the face, the top of the head may be cut off.

MCU: Medium Close Up—head and shoulders.

MS: Medium or Mid Shot—head to waist.

MLS: Medium Long Shot—head to knee.

LS: Long Shot—head to toe.

ELS: Extreme Long Shot—anything where the character is in the distance (how far away will depend on the lens being used).

STUNTS

STUNTS AND SPECIAL EFFECTS ARE THE STOCK-IN-TRADE OF HOLLYWOOD MOVIES, ESPECIALLY THE "SUMMER BLOCKBUSTERS." THE MAKERS OF THESE MEGA-BUDGET MOVIES HAVE ACCESS TO ALL THE PROFESSIONAL EXPERTISE THE INDUSTRY HAS DEVELOPED OVER THE YEARS.

Whether computer-generated (CG), stop-motion models, or huge sets with a cast of a 100 stuntmen (and women), most of the techniques were developed from low-budget films. While most of these "low-budget" films had more money than you have (at the moment), they needed ingenuity and creative thinking to find the solutions that have become the more sophisticated standards we see today.

Post-production special effects such as CGI are covered later (see pages 92–93). This section is all about in-camera effects, those that have to be created and used during the shoot.

The effects you use will be dictated by the type of film you are making. A romantic comedy ("rom-com") is not usually going to place heavy demands on your "effects department," unless you are planning to use slapstick. For this it is probably worth casting someone who can make pratfalls. It certainly makes shooting easier, and is one less extra mouth to feed. The other way is to create the effect by suggestion, using cutaways of reaction shots, or using POV (point of view) shots. This requires judicious planning,

- ▸▸ Creating in-camera effects
- ▸▸ Effects by suggestion
- ▸▸ Faking blood and gore

BLOOD AND GUTS ▼
Quentin Tarantino's films always feature liberal amounts of violence and blood. White shirts help to highlight the color of the blood but make sure it looks real. And keep a good supply of white shirts available for retakes!

shooting, and editing, but it does mean you remove the risk of anyone being hurt.

Horror movies, one of the most popular genres with the lo-no budget filmmaker, create their best scares through suggestion, especially given modern audiences' immunity to in-your-face horror. While everybody talks about how gruesome the film *Seven* is, in fact most of the crimes are not shown, but are either hinted at, described, or shown after the fact.

BLOOD ON YOUR HANDS

With horror, thriller, crime, and practically every other action-based genre, at some point you are going to need blood. Real blood, even from animals, is not a viable option, partly because it doesn't look "real," but also because it is too hard to work with. Theater blood (as in stage, not operating) can be bought, but a homemade solution is a lot more economical. A popular recipe for movie blood is shown in the box on this page.

Blood is usually accompanied by guts, or their friend, gore. Dismembered limbs will usually require the expense of prosthetics to make them look real, but spilled guts can easily be created by a visit to the local butcher, with the added bonus that if you have pets, their dinners will be provided for the week.

Once you have made copious amounts of blood, you need to find convincing ways of spilling it. These usually involve acts of extreme violence. If you decide that the subtle cut-away-shot method does not give the impact you want, you are going to have to find ways of depicting grievous bodily harm without actually causing damage to your actors, or to the sets.

People seem to find an endless range of methods for harming each other, ranging from bare hands (martial arts) to glass bottles (use sugar glass), from knives and swords to firearms, and on to bombs and automobiles. Portraying any act of violence in a film requires huge amounts of preparation and rehearsal, hopefully aided by a trained, professional stunt

SMOKE MACHINE ▲
A requirement in any action film, the smoke machine is a necessary accompaniment to any kind of explosion. Expensive to buy, they can usually be rented quite easily.

RECIPE CORNER

FAKE BLOOD

Ingredients
▸▸ Corn syrup
▸▸ Cochineal or red food coloring

These are the two main ingredients of cheap, effective blood, although lots of people add their own "secret" ingredients. As you are going to need lots of syrup, find a cash-and-carry wholesaler or source where you can buy in bulk at a reduced cost.

Method
Gently heat the syrup in a saucepan, preferably an old one or one bought just for the job, to let it thin. Add the food color until the required shade is achieved. Adding a few drops of blue food color or a small amount of espresso coffee (or strong instant equivalent) will make it darker. If you are going to use it in the mouth, only use edible products as additives.

If you are going to use it for spraying, it will need diluting with water. Just remember that it stains and will be almost impossible to remove. (Out, damned spot!)

VOMIT

Ingredients
▸▸ Carrot soup
▸▸ Blackberry jam

Method
As everyone knows, vomit often contains bits of carrot, so use some sort of carrot-based substance. One of the best is cheap carrot soup, or another cheap vegetable soup. Stir in a little blackberry jam to make it darker for screen effect. Fill up your actor's mouth and watch it flow. Be aware that the taste of the cheap soup may actually induce vomiting, so keep that camera rolling.

⬆ A plastic replica gun will work in most movies if filmed carefully, and without extreme close-ups. Just remember: The use of firearms (including disabled ones) requires proper licensed operators; even using replica guns can cause problems in some countries. The arrival of a SWAT team may not be what the scene requires, and there are plenty of tales of this happening to ill-prepared filmmakers.

coordinator. This will mean that the first thing that explodes is going to be your budget—not only for paying the stunt person but also for the all-important insurance coverage.

The simplest thing is to eliminate any big stunts—car chases, explosions, and so on—and reduce any other stunts to the minimum the story needs. Although the general rule of movie storytelling is "show, don't tell," sometimes it is easier and more powerful to imply and not show.

EVERYBODY'S KUNG-FU FIGHTING

Hong Kong–style martial arts seem to show up in every genre of movie, even when it doesn't make sense that the characters would have a knowledge of

karate. Nobody seems simply to brawl any more. If you want to include hand-to-hand combat, check out your local karate (or other martial arts) club. Their training teaches members how to pull punches convincingly, and it shouldn't be too hard to convince some of them to be in a film.

The other popular agent of violence is the firearm. If your script calls for firearms, there are several important things to consider. There is a good chance that you can get away with using replicas and adding the sounds in post-production. In some countries, even buying replica guns is restricted and requires registration, so it is advisable to look into it before you start. If you want to go for authenticity and use real guns, you are going to have to employ a licensed

SPECIAL MAKEUP EFFECTS

STEP-BY-STEP

1 Tuck some sponge into the mouth down past the lower teeth; too big a piece will look odd and hinder speech.

2 Add areas of red liner to give bruising and small cuts to the face.

3 Paint rigid collodion under the lower lip on the same side as the sponge, and press the lip down onto the collodion to stick it to the skin.

4 Color the distorted lip with black grease. Paint the roots of the teeth with red enamel.

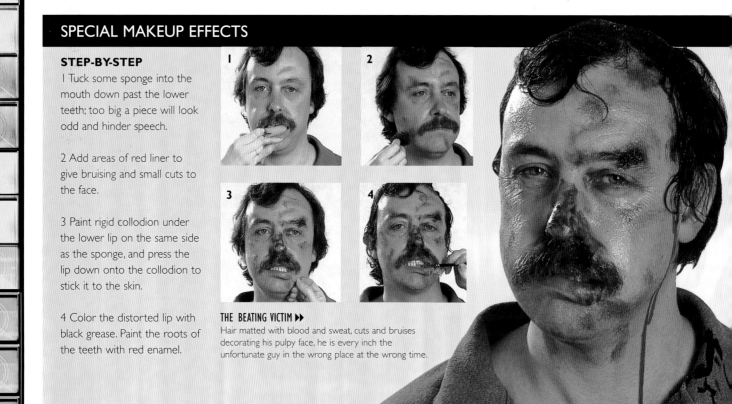

THE BEATING VICTIM ▶▶
Hair matted with blood and sweat, cuts and bruises decorating his pulpy face, he is every inch the unfortunate guy in the wrong place at the wrong time.

The flak jacket is strapped to the willing actor and the clothing is placed over the top. Cuts are put in the shirt and lightly taped together.

gun handler. They should supply all the guns you need, along with blanks (if required), and give the actors any necessary training. They should also be able to supply the squibs, the small explosives that create the blood-splattering effects of bullets entering the body.

Of course, low-budget ingenuity can overcome these perilous demands and create a decent effect with minimal danger to your actors. Exploding squibs always look impressive, if unreal, but are very dangerous. Instead of using explosives, a safer method is to use compressed air, plastic tubing, and the blood you prepared earlier. The compressed air can be either the canned variety (but this can get expensive) or one of those hand-pumped insecticide sprayers (new, of course). These are cheap and reusable. A motorized compressor is too problematic and noisy to consider.

For a more natural though less spectacular look, a small, partially inflated water balloon or condom filled with blood can be burst by someone out of shot, or by the actor pulling a thin wire across it (although theoretically, condoms are designed not to burst, whereas water balloons are). Whatever method you use, it is vital that clothing is pre-cut to let the blood seep out. Don't use your best shirt for this stunt, and keep an identical spare or two in case of retakes. It is actually a good idea to have multiple cameras at different angles for stunt shots so that they don't have to be repeated. This will also give you more coverage for the edit, which is where these effects are really made to work.

For anything involving guns, explosives, fire, or cars, always hire professional experts. Legality and safety should be your primary concerns, even if it is lo-no-budget filmmaking, and make sure you read your insurance policy properly. You're not going to finish your film if you are in prison, although it will give you plenty of time to polish your screenplay. There are a lot of things you can fake in movies, but safety and insurance aren't among them. A simple rule is: Don't ask anyone to do anything you wouldn't be prepared to do yourself.

IMPACT ZONE ⬆
The detonators are fired by either connected wires or remote control (wires are less prone to interference and accidents). The crew is placed at a safe distance, and equipment is covered to protect it from spraying "blood." The actor does not need any extra cues as the impact of the detonators is enough to tell the actor to drop to the floor, in fact it can often knock someone over.

SOUND

CONSIDERING THAT FILM IS USUALLY THOUGHT OF AS A VISUAL MEDIUM, SOUND PLAYS AN INCREDIBLY VITAL ROLE. WITH THE GENERALLY AVAILABLE TECHNOLOGY, SURROUND SOUND IS THE ONLY AFFORDABLE WAY OF ACHIEVING AN IMMERSIVE MOVIE EXPERIENCE. BAD SOUND CAN RUIN A MOVIE MORE SURELY THAN BAD IMAGES; CONVERSELY, GOOD SOUND CAN ACTUALLY RESCUE A MOVIE WITH BAD PHOTOGRAPHY.

- ▸▸ Equipment for good quality sound
- ▸▸ Dialogue and mics
- ▸▸ Ambient sound

Capturing quality sound for your movie is another craft (where technology meets art) that you will need to learn. If your film contains dialogue, you will have to record it so that the words and mouth movements match up. This is known as lip-sync[hronization]. At this early stage of your filmmaking career, foreign-language dubbing isn't going to be one of your considerations, but it is worth remembering that the actor's voices should be your primary audio interest, with as little ambient sound as possible. For this you will need the right sort of microphone (such as a Sennheiser 416 shotgun mic) and you must know

how to use it properly. Just as the quality of the lens affects the picture, so the quality of your microphone will have a huge influence on sound quality.

The mic has to be connected to a suitable recording device. With DV this is usually the camera itself. Sound is recorded digitally onto the same tape as the pictures, and as long as the mic is pointed in the right direction, with the correct recording levels, you will get sound that is as good as that produced by most other portable recording devices, and it is guaranteed to be in sync. Pro and semi-pro cameras with XLR mic inputs will not only allow you to use better microphones, but they are less susceptible to distortion. You should avoid using the camera's built-in mic, unless it is a shotgun type, as it will pick up too much ambient sound, especially that close to the camera, such as the tape drive's motor, the cameraman's movements, or even his breathing. In certain documentary situations, using the onboard mic may be unavoidable, but when working with actors, always keep the mic away from the camera.

"L.A. CASTING" O.L.

ROLL	SLATE	TAKE
9	29	2

DIR: JUST
D.O.P: R. CORNWALL
DATE 12 • 12 • '04   INT/DAY/

CLAPPER MARK ◂◂
Apart from giving a visual reference with scene and take information, the clapper board gives an audible marker to synchronize sound and pictures.

RECORDING FOR FILM

Shooting with 16mm (and 35mm) film is a different matter, and you will need a separate recording device and a way to ensure it is synched to the pictures. A simple clapperboard should do the trick, as the "clap" serves as an audible marker. The standard equipment used to be a Nagra, a small reel-to-reel tape recorder (the latest models are digital and record onto hard drives), but DAT (Digital Audio Tape) is more common these days, and very affordable. Alternatively, new portable digital recording studios such as the Tascam DP-01FX have a large internal hard drive; smaller ones such as the Zoom MRS-8 use removable SD media. Both of these devices will take XLR mics.

The power and performance of current laptops make them ideal portable digital studios. An inexpensive adapter like the Tascam US-122 (which has XLR inputs and includes Cubase recording software) will record straight onto your laptop's hard drive. And if you are shooting DV, you can also use the laptop for in-the-field editing.

HARD DISC ☜
Hard disc recorders have become a viable option for filmmakers; small portable models incorporating mixing functions and connectability with computers are now very affordable.

ADAPTER ☟
Small, inexpensive audio interfaces, such as the Tascam US-122, complete with phantom power for XLR microphones, can turn a laptop computer into a convenient recording device.

Headphone socket

USB port to connect to laptop computer

Input volume level control

XLR microphone input

DAT cassette

Tape counter and audio level monitor

XLR microphone inputs

DAT ▶▶
Portable Digital Audio Tape (DAT) recorders have replaced the Nagra as the preferred method of recording sound on movies, especially among the smaller independent filmmakers.

Record and pause buttons—the two most used during the shoot

Sound input level control

Headphone socket

RADIO MIC ▲
A tiny microphone is placed as close to the throat as possible, or sometimes hidden in the hair, and is attached to a small radio transmitter, which must be hidden out of camera view.

PALMTOP RECORDER ▼
Zoom Palm Studio is a small recording device that can be concealed on the actor and used with a small mic, instead of a radio mic.

TOP QUALITY ▶▶
A high quality microphone, such as this Sennheiser MKH 416, is expensive, but the superior sound it captures is worth the investment.

STEPPING UP TO THE MIC
Professional shotgun mics are extremely sensitive and will pick up an incredible amount of ambient sound, despite their narrow recording field. To ensure that you capture only the actors' voices, you need to have the microphone as close to them as possible. For this you need to mount the mic on a boom, a long pole that keeps it out of shot and pointed at the actors. The boom operator has to move the mic during dialogue exchanges while keeping it out of shot—not as easy as it sounds.

This works fine if you are in an enclosed environment, but shooting your characters from a distance in a crowd can present different problems. Tiny clip-on radio mics (Laveliere) are often used, but they are susceptible to interference, and are an additional expense. Portable miniDisc recorders are one solution, although transferring the digital sound to a computer, so that it remains digital, is not as simple as it should be. Another small recording device is the Zoom Palm Studio. This miniature studio records onto a SmartMedia card that can simply be mounted on the computer using an inexpensive card reader, like those used for digital stills cameras.

Apart from all the environmental sounds, shooting outdoors has the added problem of the elements, and wind in particular. This can be overcome by adding a windsock (one of those furry covers you've no doubt seen) to your mic, which silences the noise of the wind blowing across it.

A good set of headphones (cans) is as vital a part of the sound recordist's equipment as the microphone and recorder. These should be the padded, sound-insulated ones favored by music buffs. Those from your portable music player just don't block out external noise. Although you will set the levels visually using peak meters, all those unwanted sounds can only be heard by listening.

Whatever equipment or method you choose to record the sound, getting the best voice recording is paramount, especially with dramatic dialogue. Even though it is possible to rescue disasters in post-production, the actors will not always be able to recapture the intensity of the moment.

AMBIENT SOUND
Eliminating ambient sound from the voice recording starts with keeping people on the set quiet. This is relatively easy as they (should) understand the importance of a noise-free recording. All mobile phones have to be switched off. Some people put theirs into silent mode, but if radio mics are being used, the phones can interfere with the signal (as can taxis and emergency vehicles, but there is nothing to

HEADPHONES ▶▶
Quality headphones will block out external noise and allow you to clearly hear a full dynamic range of sounds. Try to match the quality of the headphones with that of your microphone.

Slate	Take	Timecode	Description
1	WT		
	WT	00:11	
	1	01:25	Girl shouting "Dad"
	2	03:12	Deep breathing for opening
3	3	03:32	Atmos
	1	03:53	
	2	04:18	
	3	04:49	Atmos
2	4	05:04	
	1	05:45	
4	WT	06:33	
	1	08:50	Girl's breakfast dial
4a	2	10:07	
	1	10:47	Blanket and laughter
	2	11:29	
5	WT	12:14	
	1	12:57	
	2	14:09	
	3	15:35	Atmos + dial
	4	17:17	
6	WT	19:03	
7	1	20:38	
8	1	23:52	
	1	25:25	Atmos
	2	30:07	Atmos + cereal in bowl
	3	30:45	Cereal in bowl
	WT	31:12	
		31:37	

⬆ The sound recordist's log should contain similar information to that of the camera person, except with additional wildtrack (WT) or atmos takes, causing the timecode to differ slightly.

be done about those. Unfortunately, the rest of the world won't come to a standstill while you record a take).

Apart from judicious placement of the mic, there are measures you can take to eliminate any extraneous noise, and most of them involve common sense. For example, don't shoot your film under a flight path, next to a major road or highway, near emergency services, schools, or railroads—you get the idea. Cities are incredibly noisy places and unless you need that continual urban hum, try to find places or times when it is at a minimum. Sundays and public holidays are good, and may be the only times you and your crew are free anyway.

Although you are making every effort to remove all extraneous sound, you are still going to need some, depending on your movie, of course. All those

Headphones: for monitoring recording

Boom pole: Lightweight and extendable

Recording device: Usually a DAT or digital hard disk recorder. The case is designed for transport and easy operation on location

Windshield prevents or muffles noise caused by wind

SOUND ON LOCATION ⬆

With lightweight recording devices it is possible for the sound recorder to double as the boom holder. Having control of the microphone makes it easier to ensure optimum sound as the recorder has instant monitoring of the recording through the headphones.

sound effects like footsteps, doors shutting, and car engines have to be included, as well as general noise. In our daily lives we don't usually notice these sounds, or simply shut them out—they become conspicuous only by their absence. A scene without any ambient noise would seem flat and unnatural, so it has to be recorded, preferably while on location. Use your standard sound-recording equipment, announcing what the sound is and for which scene/slate. Also keep a written note of what you have recorded.

If you are using a DV camera, the easiest method is to place the slate in front of the lens with a note of the sound you are recording. This can be imported into your editing software, along with the rest of your footage.

Record everything you think you will need, as clearly as possible, but anything you miss can be added in post-production (see pages 96–97).

DIRECTING

THE ROLE OF DIRECTOR IS SEEN AS ONE OF THE MORE GLAMOROUS AND PRESTIGIOUS IN THE FILM INDUSTRY. DIRECTORS ARE CONSIDERED THE CREATIVE GENIUSES BEHIND A FILM, AS IT IS THEIR VISION THAT BRINGS IT TO THE SCREEN.

- ▸▸ Communicating your vision
- ▸▸ Working with talent
- ▸▸ Calling the shots
- ▸▸ The director's role

Although there is a certain amount of truth in this romantic notion, a lot of the director's time is taken up in mundane administrative matters, and the larger the production, the more decisions a director must make. In military terms, a director is like a general, responsible for strategy, giving orders, and overseeing the troops.

AUTEURS

There are two specific types of director, independent of personality traits. Writer-directors are the elite, the auteurs of the film world, who take a film from conception to completion. They have a story to tell and a vision of how it should be told on screen. The other type will take a screenplay and use their vision to interpret how it should be played out. Not all directors are capable of writing an original script, and even fewer writers have the personality needed to command a film crew.

Most first-time filmmakers tend to jump in as writer-directors. They want to make a film and usually have an idea for the story they want to tell, and this is as it should be. That story might be an adaptation, or one inspired by another story, but whatever the source, novice directors will have ideas they want to manifest. No matter how multitalented or multitasking he or she is, to bring the concept to reality the director will need to enlist the help of others in the form of actors. It is the director's job to coax the best performances possible out of that talent.

The director's work with the actors begins with casting and auditions (see pages 38–41), and continues through into rehearsals. These are vital for establishing relationships between the actors—and with the director. It is the relationship between the director and the actors that will determine how good a performance the latter will give.

TOP FIVE DIRECTORIAL QUALITIES

1 **Vision** Translating what is on paper into a moving image on the screen, and coming up with creative interpretations for both visuals and performances.

2 **Organization** Making sure everyone and everything is in the right place at the right time, or at least delegating someone to take care of this.

3 **Diplomacy and communication** Knowing the best way to deal with people (cast and crew in particular) in order to get them to do what you want without upsetting them.

4 **Knowledge** Having a good knowledge of all aspects of the film production cycle, or at least enough to recognize when and where problems may arise.

5 **Humility** It would probably set a precedent, but this quality would certainly make the above four work more smoothly.

Actor: The director has to coax the best possible performances from the cast, whether physical or emotional. It is important to allow time for the actors to warm up, but without delaying the schedule.

Director (Quentin Tarantino): Explains his vision for the shot to the cast and crew.

DoP: Has to visually interpret the director's ideas and capture them on film or video. His relationship with the director must be symbiotic.

Fight/stunt coordinator: Has to choreograph the action scenes in action films, hire stunt people, and train the actors. Safety is one of his primary concerns, even beyond getting the shot.

TWO OF A KIND

There are two extremes of directors—the total control freak and go-with-the-flow type—but you should aim to be somewhere in between. The control-freak director will want the actors to move and speak exactly as they are instructed, treating them as no more than puppets. The go-with-the-flow director will let the actors improvise as much as they want, often to the detriment of the original script. What is needed is for the director to allow the actors to explore their characters and make suggestions, tempering this with clarity of vision. Directors must find ways of communicating their perception of the character to the actors so they will be able to understand how the character would behave in the given situations.

NOT MAKING IT BIG

Many actors come with stage training and experience, if any at all, where actions and voices have to be "big."

This does not work on film, where the proximity of the camera demands understatement, and exchanges between actors have to be more intimate and often more intense. But these are not the only differences. In movies, actors do not have to learn and recite huge chunks of dialogue. With scenes shot out of sequence, and multiple takes for coverage, it can demand a lot of energy for an actor to maintain focus on the character, which is why directors have to be empathetic with their talent, praising their efforts while finding diplomatic ways of getting exactly what they want.

One of the best ways is to talk to the character, that is, to address the actor as the character. Ask characters questions about their actions in order to elicit the appropriate emotion or response. The other method to use is, "That was great but can we just try…." In the end a lot of it is about developing interpersonal skills, and understanding each actor individually. What will work with one actor won't

GO WITH THE FLOW ⊻

Try making yourself a flowchart like this, on your computer. If you can add To Do lists and contacts it will make the whole organization of your shoot easier. Or give it to your producer to do.

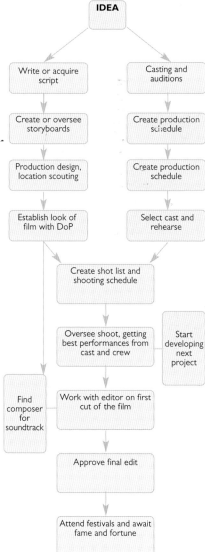

```
                    IDEA
          ┌──────────┴──────────┐
   Write or acquire          Casting and
       script                 auditions
          │                      │
  Create or oversee      Create production
     storyboards             schedule
          │                      │
 Production design,      Create production
  location scouting          schedule
          │                      │
  Establish look of        Select cast and
    film with DoP             rehearse
          └──────────┬──────────┘
              Create shot list and
               shooting schedule
                      │
           Oversee shoot, getting        Start
           best performances from     developing
               cast and crew             next
                      │                 project
    Find      Work with editor on first
  composer           cut of the film
    for
 soundtrack
                      │
               Approve final edit
                      │
             Attend festivals and await
                 fame and fortune
```

SHOT LIST ◀◀
Keeping an accurate list of every shot and its relativity to the script is vital for making the editor's job easier. Any script changes are also noted, as the shooting script and the written script may differ.

Directing note for actors

Something to be discussed with DoP

Note for editor

Dialogue change

Directing note for actors

More shooting notes to be added to shooting list

work with another. Unfortunately, it is something that can only be learned through trial and error, and experience. A lot of actors and directors continually work together because they understand, and respect, each other. If you can establish that sort of relationship, your movies will develop in ways that you could not imagine.

Directing isn't just about drawing the right emotions out of the actors; you have to do it in relation to the camera. This means orchestrating the movement of the actors in front of the camera while maintaining control over framing and the movement of the camera itself.

When it comes to cinematography, some directors are very hands-on, often operating the camera at the same time as directing the actors. This allows the director to make snap decisions about composition,

▲ SCRIPT CAPTIONS AND NOTES
No matter how many amends a script has before the shoot, on the actual day the director can still make changes, especially if he wrote it. Although amends will appear on the shooting log pages, making notes on the script will help during the editing process. Write plenty of notes because, with so much happening, you may forget what you did or why. The script on the left is untouched, while the one on the right has the director's notes and amends.

GETTING THE SHOT ◀◀
Once explained by the director, the DoP will position the camera ready to shoot, while the director checks the shot on a field monitor (if available). The makeup artist applies the special effect just before the shot.

TALKING IT THROUGH ⬆
The director will discuss the shot with the DoP/cameraman, explaining precisely what he wants.

which works well on lo-no-budget shoots where video-assist isn't available. It also speeds up the process, as the need to explain everything to the DoP or camera-operator is eliminated, as is the need for extra retakes.

One of the perceived problems of filming and directing at the same time is the difficulty of giving enough attention to what the actors are doing. Much of this depends on how comfortable you are behind the lens. It also depends on how much faith you have in your actors. If you have rehearsed with the actors and are pleased with their performance, then just shoot it. One advantage of video is that you can shoot and shoot, but it is also a disadvantage, because with film there is more of an incentive to make sure that the take is right the first time.

As the director, you have to decide what needs to be shot in terms of coverage—establishing shots, medium shots, close-ups, and cutaways. Again, with video you can get plenty of coverage, as much as your cast and crew will tolerate. With film you have to be very clear about what you are going to need because every foot you shoot is going to cost you, not just for stock but also for developing and telecine.

CALL TO ACTION

All the pre-production meetings, the rehearsals with actors, and the hours of overseeing setups culminate in the moment when the director gets to call "Action!" There is actually a protocol that has to be followed before those words are shouted, depending on the equipment.

From this point on, the director is in charge, and everything carries on until he calls "Cut!" The DoP is the only other person permitted to call "Cut!" and only if there is a technical fault with the camera or lights. Even if an actor misses his or her lines, it is the director's decision whether to continue with the take or start again. Once he has called "Cut!" the director decides if he or she is happy with the take, and will check with the DoP that the shot was technically OK. A good director will usually praise the actors if it was a good take, and may ask them if they were pleased with it, as a courtesy. Generally, a director should not ask the cast or crew for their opinion of the take, as this can undermine his authority. If there is any doubt, the director may decide to reshoot, making any suggestions to the actors on ways to improve the scene. If the actors, who are notoriously self-critical, are happy, the director will often let it go and shoot the scene from a different angle or with a different lens.

And so it goes on, setup after setup, until there is enough footage in the can to call it a wrap and move on to the next stage—sorting through everything and putting it together in a coherent manner.

CATERING

YOU MAY BE WONDERING WHAT CATERING HAS TO DO WITH FILMMAKING, BUT IT IS ONE OF THE FEW JOBS WHERE THE PROVERBIAL FREE LUNCH ACTUALLY EXISTS. IN THE EARLY DAYS OF HOLLYWOOD, BECAUSE FILMS WERE OFTEN SHOT MILES AWAY FROM TOWNS, CATERING WAGONS WERE SENT TO THE LOCATION, AND THE TRADITION HAS REMAINED.

▸▸ The free lunch

▸▸ Food = energy

▸▸ Drinks and snacks

SUSTENANCE ON THE SET ▸▸

If you aren't paying your cast and crew a lot of money, at least you should be keeping them well fed. The menu near right would probably cause a mutiny after the first day. Treat your people kindly and make an effort to provide good quality food and drink, and you'll notice an increase in the energy they'll give to your production.

HOW NOT TO FEED YOUR CAST & CREW

Breakfast:
• Cold coffee, cold tea, warm cola, cornflakes, sour milk.

Lunch:
• Cheese sandwiches, water, and the leftover coffee and tea from breakfast.

Dinner:
• Don't you people have homes to go to? It's late, I'm tired, and you have to be back here in five hours.

AN EXCELLENT MENU FOR A LOCATION WITH NO POWER SUPPLY

Breakfast:
• Cereals, bread, sliced cold meat (for example, ham), croissants or muffins, fruit juice, and fresh fruit (apples, pears, bananas). Hot tea (including herbal) and coffee. (Use vacuum flasks to keep water hot.)

Snacks:
• Dried fruit and nuts, chocolate bars, fresh fruits, water, juices, and soft drinks. Tea and coffee.

Lunch:
• Antipasti: Cooked and/or cured ham, salami, olives, sundried tomatoes, grilled peppers and eggplant (aubergine), grissini (bread sticks).
• Pasta tricolore (see recipe opposite).
• Cold roast chicken.
• Fresh fruits.

Dinner:
• If the day's shoot finishes after 8pm, think about going to a local restaurant to eat.

Even with a small- to medium-sized cast and crew, feeding everyone on set has the very practical advantage of stopping people from wandering off and holding up the schedule. Running a film shoot is about being in charge, and deciding when and where your crew eats is part of that responsibility. On location shoots, where you will be facing time constraints either from the fading light or the property owners wanting to regain their premises, it is even more important.

On the lo-no-budget film, where you have persuaded most people to work for nothing, the least you can do is feed them, and there are plenty of ways to do this without blowing your nonexistent budget. Deciding what to feed them is also important. For example, pasta is cheap, easy to make, and filling. The carbohydrates will give your crew the energy they need to keep working, but if you give them too much, it may actually slow them down.

Your location may make it impossible actually to prepare food, and you may not want to carry all the necessary supplies and equipment anyway. Getting a friend or relative to prepare the food and bring it to the set is one possible solution. Although this may limit you to cold food, it can be more imaginative than cheese sandwiches. When you are scouting locations, check out the restaurants (eat-in and take-out) in the area. Use your charm to arrange a special discount deal in exchange for a credit or plug in your film. It is important that the food is brought to the set, or someone will have to stay behind to guard the equipment and the setup.

It is also a good idea to find out about the crew's dietary demands and preferences. You may not be able to please everyone, but if you know all their food foibles you can try to provide a reasonable balance.

Provide a good supply of drinks, both hot and cold. Caffeine is a staple of any film set, whether it is from coffee, tea, or soda. How practical it is to keep hot drinks on the set will depend on your situation, but plenty of fresh water, fruit juices, and cola are easy to provide. Just make sure all liquids are kept away from the equipment; there's no quicker way to destroy your gear than mixing it with sugary liquids. Under no circumstances serve alcohol during any part of the shoot; it does not enhance creativity or performance.

Snacks are a good idea. There can be a lot of time during set-ups when people have nothing to do. Fruit is excellent and practical (apples and bananas especially). Try to avoid anything too sticky that will transfer from fingers to equipment, and keep plenty of paper towels on hand as an extra preventive measure.

This may sound more like *Good Housekeeping* than good filmmaking but, in the words of Bob Marley, "A hungry mob is an angry mob." Tempers will fray when blood sugar is low, and it's not as if there aren't already enough fragile egos for you to deal with. Mealtimes are also a great way to release some of the pressure of work, and let cast and crew talk informally.

When the shoot is over, especially if you have been supplying a minimal lunch, treat everyone to a big meal, whether it's in your home or at a restaurant. It's gestures like these that will help ensure that people will work for you again. Film producer Ishmail Merchant (of Merchant Ivory Productions) was also renowned as an excellent cook and he used this as leverage to get top actors to work for lower rates, just because they wanted to eat his food. It goes to show just how important providing good food is for the low-budget filmmaker.

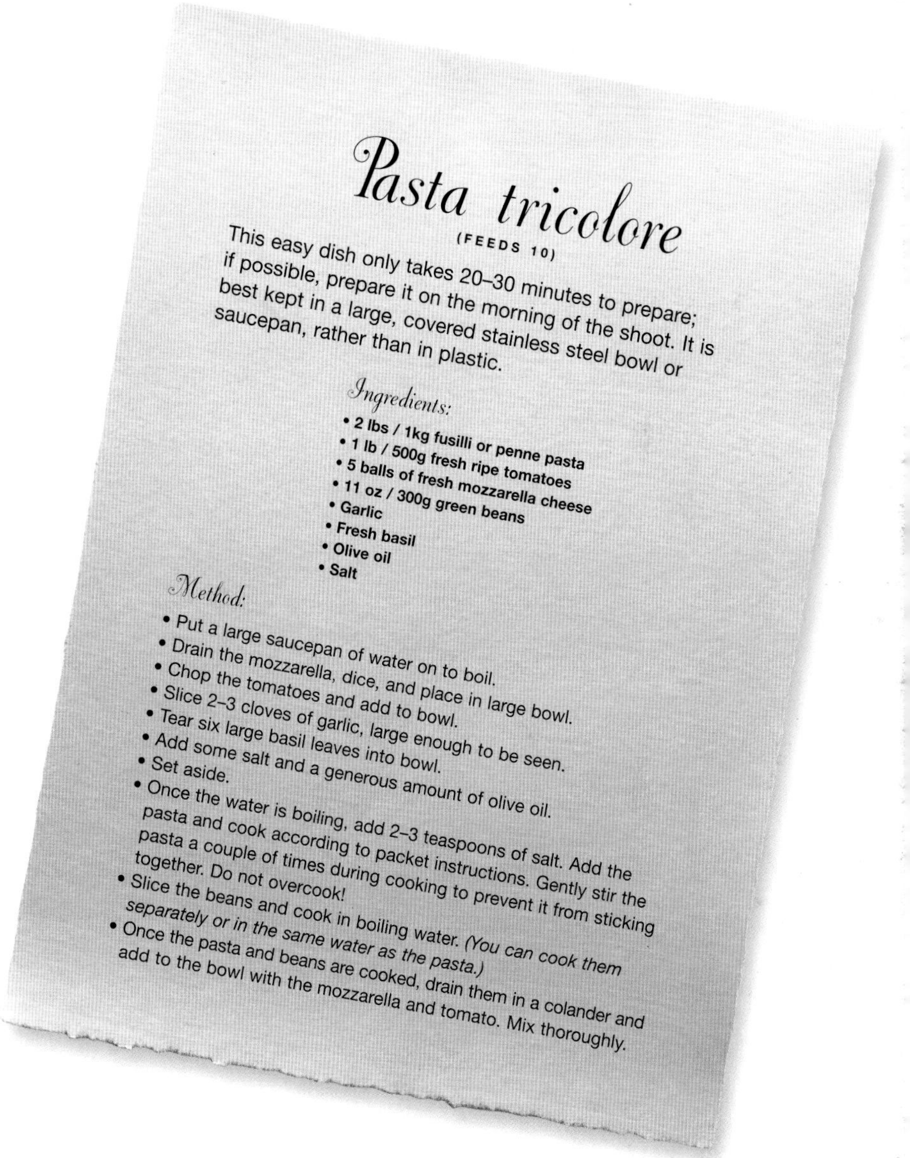

Pasta tricolore

(FEEDS 10)

This easy dish only takes 20–30 minutes to prepare; if possible, prepare it on the morning of the shoot. It is best kept in a large, covered stainless steel bowl or saucepan, rather than in plastic.

Ingredients:

- **2 lbs / 1kg fusilli or penne pasta**
- **1 lb / 500g fresh ripe tomatoes**
- **5 balls of fresh mozzarella cheese**
- **11 oz / 300g green beans**
- **Garlic**
- **Fresh basil**
- **Olive oil**
- **Salt**

Method:

- Put a large saucepan of water on to boil.
- Drain the mozzarella, dice, and place in large bowl.
- Chop the tomatoes and add to bowl.
- Slice 2–3 cloves of garlic, large enough to be seen.
- Tear six large basil leaves into bowl.
- Add some salt and a generous amount of olive oil.
- Set aside.
- Once the water is boiling, add 2–3 teaspoons of salt. Add the pasta and cook according to packet instructions. Gently stir the pasta a couple of times during cooking to prevent it from sticking together. Do not overcook!
- Slice the beans and cook in boiling water. *(You can cook them separately or in the same water as the pasta.)*
- Once the pasta and beans are cooked, drain them in a colander and add to the bowl with the mozzarella and tomato. Mix thoroughly.

DON'T BLOW THE BUDGET ▲
Try this inexpensive and simple recipe for the perfect solution to the "free lunch."

POST-PRODUCTION

Once everything is in the can, that is, when the shooting is finished, it is time to start putting all the pieces together. Compared to the shoot, this is a long, drawn-out process, but a vital one if your film is going to attract an audience—and keep it.

During post-production everything you shot will be edited into a cohesive whole, sounds will be added and mixed with any music you want to include, additional special effects can be inserted, as will the all-important titles and credits. The process finishes with the final tweaks, such as color grading, before outputting to the finished medium.

These are all jobs you can do on your own, although enlisting the help of someone experienced in the different fields, even in an advisory capacity, may help the job to run more smoothly and rapidly.

As with the shoot, proper planning and systematic working methods will make the process a lot easier without hindering the spontaneity of the creative process. It is to be hoped that the rigors of pre-production and the production itself haven't left you exhausted and jaded, but it is advisable to take a short break from the movie, even just a couple of days, before immersing yourself in post-production. This will let you look at what you've shot with fresher eyes.

As nearly all post-production work is done digitally these days, this section concentrates on a digital workflow using the best and most affordable tools on the market. However, as in any pursuit, it is the craftsperson and not the tools that determines the quality of the work.

TELECINE

IF FILM IS YOUR CHOSEN MEDIUM, YOU WILL NEED TO FIND A RELIABLE LAB, ONE THAT WILL NOT ONLY PROCESS YOUR PRECIOUS STOCK BUT ALSO PROVIDE A RANGE OF ANCILLARY SERVICES SUCH AS TELECINE, COLOR GRADING, AND PRINTING.

- ▸ Development labs
- ▸ Negotiating a deal
- ▸ Specialized developing

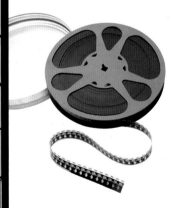

RUSHES ▲
Rushes are still sent as film prints on large-budget productions, although digital is now the preferred format.

No matter how much care you take loading and unloading film, and with lighting and exposure during the shoot, if the lab messes up the developing there's not a lot you can do but reshoot. If you're lucky, the lab will replace the film but, unless you are properly insured, you will have to bear the brunt of the reshoot costs.

Even in major moviemaking centers there are only a few development labs, so you should approach all of them and try to negotiate a good package deal. Being a student, or having a registered student on your crew, is a sure-fire way of keeping the cost down. Once you have quotes from all the labs, pick one and use it for the whole project—unless it seriously messes up. That means using it for developing, telecine, work prints, and any other processes you might need, such as blow-ups. Establishing a good relationship with a lab will make everything run more smoothly, and it is more likely to help you when you are in a jam, although this can take a long time. Don't go into a lab expecting or, worse, demanding preferential treatment for your first film. In fact, some labs will give good deals to novice filmmakers in the hope of retaining their business and discouraging them from going over to video.

When you take your film to the lab, you should attach a shooting list, with any notes or developing instructions. The more information you give, the better. There's no shame in asking questions, so find out what the lab wants in order to get the best results with your footage. And footage is what it will want to know about because that is how you will be charged—by the foot.

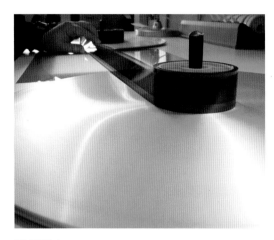

LAB WORK ▲
To get the best results from telecine, a quality-controlled lab environment with expert operators is recommended.

After you've handed your precious freshly exposed film over to the lab, and any sound tapes, the first things you will get back are the rushes. These can be ungraded prints with the sound striped on for making rough edits and general checks that you got all the shots, that they are clean, and properly exposed. The alternative is to get your rushes telecined. Put simply, this is the process of copying film onto videotape so that it can either be viewed on a television or transferred to a computer for editing (see pages 86–91).

SUPER 8

Finding labs to deal with 16mm and 35mm film is fairly easy, but what about Super 8? Although the format still has a dedicated following, video camcorders more or less killed it off as a viable commercial consumer venture. Kodak still develops its Kodachrome positive film, using a mail-in service (included in the film's price). Some larger labs will develop negative Super 8 stock, such as Kodak's Vision

CAMERA REPORT ▸▸

This sheet has to be filled in by the camera operator, or assistant, during the shoot. The completed form is then taped to the film can. These are usually produced in triplicate—one for the lab, one for the producer, and one for the editor—and are supplied by the lab, each having its own style of form.

1. Include as much data about the camera and film as possible. This will help the lab with processing.

2. Slate/scene and take numbers must match those on the clapperboard/slate.

3. Counter reading (or dial) is taken from the camera's footage meter. This will also tell you the amount of footage used for each take.

4. Lens and Stop helps with exposure and depth of field issues.

5. Print tells which shots are useable and should be printed for editing. With telecine it is often easier to simply transfer the whole reel.

6. Information about lighting and filters will help with color grading later in the process. Any other relevant notes about the shoot can be added here, such as pushing the film.

7. This tells how much film was used, wasted, or unexposed (short end), and is used for calculating costs.

8. Information about the telecine. This is often put on a separate form and would also include details about sound and timecodes.

CAMERA REPORT

1 Production Company: THALI BROTHERS Date: 29/2/05 Sheet No: 1 of 1
Job Title: TIN PLATE FRATERNITY Studio/Location: LOCATION
Camera Operator: AL CHIARASCURO Director: ALAN SMITHEE Assistant: BEN DOVER

Camera Model: ARRI SR Mag No:
Load Length: 400'
Colour ☑ / B & W □ Negative □ / Positive ☑ Stock No: 5246 Code No: 2508 Roll No: 1 of 1 Emulsion No: 513/014
□ 35mm □ Super 35 □ 16mm □ Super16 ☑ Super8 □

2 Slate/Scene	Take No	3 Counter Reading	Take Length	4 Lens & Stop	5 Print (P)	6 Essential Information (Filters, Lighting etc)
1	1	0'	30'	f2.8 25mm	P	
	2	30'	30'	↓ ↓	P	EXT DAY
	3	60'	10'	↓	P	ND 0.6
2	4	70	30'	↓	P	
	2	100'	25'	f4	P	
	3	125'	25'	85mm	P	
3	1	150'	30'	↓ ↓	P	
	2	180	50'	f4 18mm	P	
4	1	230'	50'	↓ ↓	P	
	2	280'	30'	f2.8 25mm	P	
	3	310'	30'	↓ ↓	P	
		340'	20'	↓ ↓	P	
		360'				

7 Total exposed 360' Short ends _____ Waste 40' To Print 320'

WORK PRINT ☑ lab normal
TELECINE PREP □ one-light transfer □ one-light - timed to _____
FRAMING: □ 4:3 □ 4:3 letterbox ☑ best light transfer □ best-light □ fully timed
Film to tape transfer speed: □ 24 fps ☑ 1.66 □ 1.78 □ 1.85 □ scene-to-scene transfer
PAL □ NTSC ☑ □ Betacam SP ☑ 25 fps □ 30 fps □ other □ 16:9 anamorphic □ other
8 □ DigiBeta □ DVCAM small □ DVCAM big Match back to film Yes □ No ☑
Special delivery and invoice instructions □ MiniDV ☑

---

working with Kodachrome—you can do an offline edit on computer, cutting the film only when you are satisfied. Remember that with Kodachrome there is only one projectable original. There are also devices for home use that transfer film to video, but you would have to be shooting a lot of film to justify the cost, and have plenty of time to experiment to get optimum results.

If you want to work with film, 16mm and up, then find a good lab and services facility and stick with it. The same is true if you want to use Super 8, but you are going to have to rely more heavily on the telecine and resolve to finish your movie digitally. On top of all that, you must realize that you have to pay for these services, and keep paying.

range, as a special order, but it isn't likely you will get overnight development of a single roll. Telecine is less of a problem. Most telecine facilities will be able to do a professional digital transfer. Given the lack of suitable projection for Super 8, staying with a high-grade digital transfer is the best option.

There are also places that specialize in archiving old home movies to video. It is advisable to check out the quality of the transfer before committing your film, but their prices are considerably lower than other labs. This could be an ideal solution if you are

CHECK THESE OUT

www.digitalcopycat.com Low-cost UK film-to-video transfer

www.pro8mm.com Supplier of Super 8 film, processing, and telecine based in California

www.tfgtransfer.com Economical telecine services for 16mm and 35mm

www.filmcraftlab.com Telecine services in US Midwest

www.super8transfers.com UK-based telecine for Super 8 filmmakers

www.superdailies.com Californian telecine service

www.kftv.com/product-7140.html List of international telecine services

EDITING

ONCE YOUR MOVIE HAS BEEN SHOT AND IS "IN THE CAN," YOU HAVE TO COLLECT ALL THE PIECES TOGETHER AND PUT THEM INTO AN ORDER THAT IS NOT ONLY COHERENT BUT ALSO HAS THE RHYTHM AND PACING TO CAPTURE AN AUDIENCE. BAD EDITING CAN RUIN YOUR MOVIE, JUST AS GOOD EDITING CAN SOMETIMES RESCUE A BAD SHOOT, BUT PROPER PLANNING AND ORGANIZATION SHOULD MEAN THAT NEITHER SITUATION OCCURS.

LOG ON ⬇
Keeping an accurate list of all your shots will make the whole editing process that much easier, especially during the initial stages.

▶▶ Importance of the shoot log

▶▶ First assembly and rough cut

▶▶ Final cut

CAPTURED ▶▶
To upload the footage to your computer, connect the camera using a FireWire (iLink, IEEE-1394) lead. You will now be able to control the camera through the software. In Final Cut (Express and Pro) you can enter all the information from your log sheet into each clip as you capture it.

This planning starts during pre-production. If you are going to bring in an experienced editor, get their input when you are writing up your shooting list. He or she will be able to tell you what sort of shots will be needed for the edit. If you intend to do your own editing, you will have to consider how much coverage you will need to shoot with establishing shots, close-ups, inserts, and cutaways. Some of these you may not decide on until the day of the shoot, but bear in mind the importance of having a wide variety of shots and angles.

During the shoot, keep an accurate list of every shot, with reel number, timecode, description, and an indication of the shot's usability. Logging all the shots means that you can practically do a paper edit without looking at a single image. A paper edit is simply the process of taking all the logged information and putting it in the right order; when it comes to capturing the images from the tape to your computer, you will know exactly where to find them, and the order in which they need to be placed, saving hours of searching through tapes looking for a shot. That does not mean you should ignore or disregard all the other footage. There may be a certain look or a phrase that the actor delivers in an otherwise rejected take that can be inserted.

With digital shoots the editor could even be on set and, using a laptop, start assembling a rough cut right away. Any inserts or pick-ups that need to be shot can be done immediately, rather than calling the actors back later. Whether you can convince an editor to do this is another matter. If you are directing and intend to edit as well, then working like that will be

ROLL #	SLATE #	TAKE	TIMECODE	OK	SHOT DESCRIPTION
1	1	1	00:02		ECU OF man's face WA
		2	00:18	✓	"
		3	00:35	✓	"
	3	1	00:55	✓	MCU of bed WA
		2	01:18		
		3	01:28	✓	
		4	02:01	✓	
	2	1	02:40	✓	CU Girl's face WA
	4	1	04:51	✓	MS overhead of bed
		2	05:24	✓	
	49	1	05:57	✓	MS/WIDE ON TRACK SHOT OF COUCH
		2	06:35	✓	
	5	1	07:15	✓	MC STEADICAM MX SHOT 7
		2	08:35		
		3	09:07	✓	
		4	10:47	✓	
	6	1	12:01	✓	CU of wife
	7	1	13:24	✓	MS of man preparing food
	8	1	17:51	✓	CU of cereal in bowl

→72

The camera is controlled by these buttons.

Enter information about the clip in these boxes.

Once all the clips have been captured into the "bin," you can start making your rough edit by dropping all the clips onto the Timeline in approximately the order you want.

Project browser window, where all the clips are stored and the various filters and effects can be accessed.

Viewer, for previewing clips stored in the browser window.

Canvas window is for viewing clips in the timeline.

Timeline, where all the clips are placed for chopping and enhancing.

Video timeline: The DV clips are split into their audio and video components, with support for an unlimited number of video tracks, to allow complex editing and experimentation.

Audio timeline: Final Cut Express allows for 99 audio tracks, which should be more than enough for even the most complex movie.

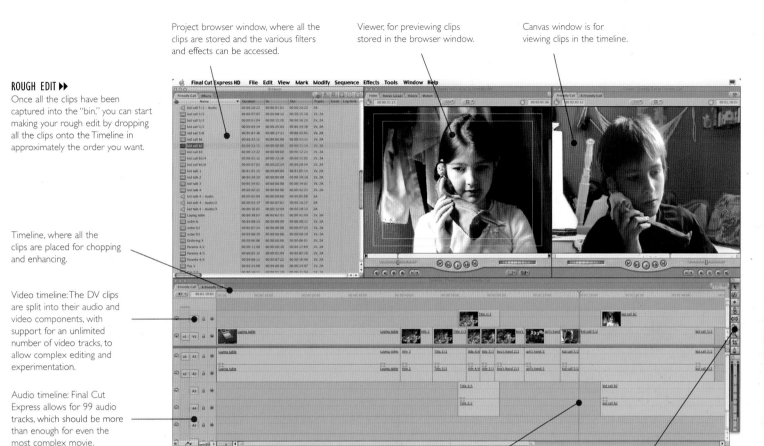

The playhead shows where on the timeline you are, and what is being shown in the canvas window.

The tool palette and audio meters: all the tools for performing precise and complex edits.

impractical, but as the director/editor you should be aware of exactly what you need.

FIRST CUT IS THE DEEPEST

The initial stage of editing is known as the first assembly, when all the material from the shoot, visual and audio, is put together in a very loose format, possibly based on a paper edit. Assuming you are working with digital video (either directly or through telecine), you will be using a non-linear editor (NLE) such as Final Cut, Premiere, or Avid. The first assembly amounts to uploading all the material onto your computer, into "bins" in the software, labeling

everything so that it makes sense and can be put into an order that resembles the chronology of the script.

From this, a rough cut is made. The material from the first assembly is put into an order that starts to resemble an actual movie. Even at this stage, a movie intended to be only 10 minutes long can run for 15 or 20 minutes, but, as the name implies, these are rough cuts, still with plenty of fat on them.

The editor will slice away at a rough cut until it is much closer to the final length, bringing in the director to give approval (assuming that the roles have been split). Many DVD re-releases are marketed as "director's cuts," but this "first-cut" stage is really the

ROLL ON ▶▶
Final Cut, like other NLEs, is non-destructive, so clips can be quickly shortened or lengthened simply by dragging the end. The changes are shown instantly in the canvas window.

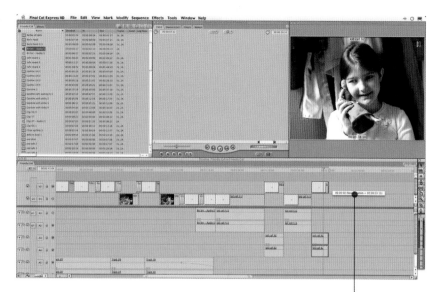

director's cut, as it is the one that is approved before being tweaked and fine-tuned to the best of the editor's ability. Depending on the level of the director's involvement, even a rough cut could be called a director's cut.

FROM FINE TO FINAL CUT

Once the director and producer have approved the cut, it is up to the editor to tighten the edit. This involves shaving off excess seconds or minutes, tightening transitions, and establishing the film's rhythm. The shorter the film, the more difficult this can be. Each cut has to be tighter and tell more of the story. As a generation brought up on MTV, we are used to short, fast cuts in music videos and commercials, and to a certain extent these techniques can be transferred to narrative films. It's all about the pacing of your film. Action and thriller films will work better with quick cuts, while moodier or romantic movies will work better with longer cuts. Either way, it is always best to avoid unnecessarily long shots and to reduce the overall length of your film in order to maintain the viewer's interest.

However you cut it, once everyone (editor, director, producer—who may all be you) is satisfied with the visuals, the titles, sound effects, and final music score can be added to give what is known as the final cut. If you've shot on film and have been editing a digitized (telecine) version, you will have to create an EDL (editing decision list) for the negative cutter to follow. Top-end editing software, such as Apple's Final Cut Pro, Adobe Premiere Pro, and Avid, will generate these automatically. Digital-video shoots, on the other hand, are ready for printing the final cut back to a distribution tape or for burning onto a DVD.

CREATIVE EDITING

How you edit your movie is dictated not only by what you have shot but also by how you use it. When Robert Rodriguez made *El Mariachi* (1992), he shot

Dragging the edge of the clip will shorten or lengthen it. The time is shown in the yellow strip.

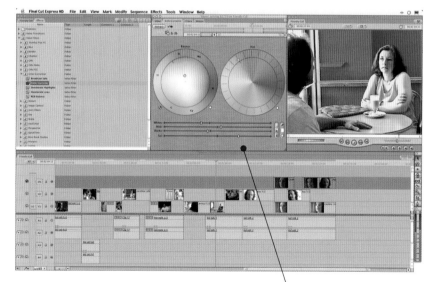

COLOR CORRECTION ▲
Even with the best cinematographer in the world, you are never going to get consistent color. Shooting DV guerrilla-style, you have no chance. Ideally, you need a calibrated production monitor to do accurate correction, but even doing it on your computer monitor will make a huge difference to the look of your movie. Because you can adjust individual clips, you can create different looks for each character, if you want.

Dragging the sliders adjusts contrast, saturation, and balance.

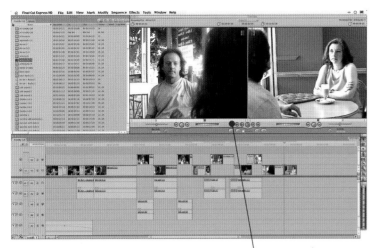

NEAT AND TRIM ▲

Cuts often have to be frame accurate. This scene was shot with two cameras, which meant that the action had to be aligned as accurately as possible. This window shows the two frames either side of the cut, which can be fine-tuned using the buttons in the window.

Fine control of the cut is done with these buttons.

Fine tune the amount and length of the transition in this window.

Tracks can be switched on and off (hidden) with this button.

PRACTICE LINE ▲

With unlimited video tracks it is easy to try alternative edits, leaving the other ones intact. Tracks can be switched off by clicking on the green film icon on the left side of the track.

Sound levels are adjusted by clicking and dragging on the volume line.

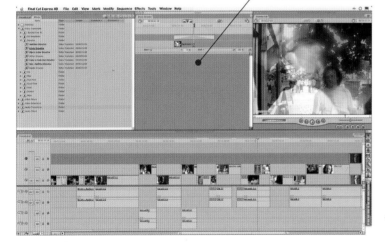

TRANSITIONS ▲

The use of transitions is best kept to a minimum, especially some of the more "fancy" ones. Cross dissolves, or fades, can work well if used with discretion. Simply drop the transition onto the timeline between the two clips and adjust the length and amount.

all the action on a 16mm camera without sync sound. He recorded the dialogue immediately after the shoot on a portable cassette recorder. When it came to editing, as soon as the dialogue started going out of sync, he inserted another shot—either a reaction shot, a close-up, or a cutaway, anything that allowed him to get the sound and picture back together. The editing was done out of necessity, a creative solution to a technical problem, but it gave the picture added pace and tension.

Working with a digital NLE, you get lots of video and audio tracks so you can layer all your shots. And it is easy to experiment with different cuts because the editing is non-destructive. Shots can be lengthened and shortened at will, and played back immediately.

Even with all the latest technology, editing is still a long and drawn-out process and, like any creative venture, as soon as you have finished you will see a way it could be improved.

SOUND BALANCE ▲

Although a dedicated sound program will do a better job, it is still possible to improve and balance the sound levels in Final Cut Express. It is not up to the standard of the Pro version, but that dialogue you didn't quite record properly will definitely improve.

POST-PRODUCTION

EDITING SOFTWARE ◀◀
Apple's entry level editing software, iMovie, included on every new Mac, is very capable and simple to use. If you don't need lots of sound and video tracks, it works. More than one cinema-released indy movie has been edited with it.

Clips are stored here and dragged to the timeline.

Preview window

Timeline

Clips are stored here.

Preview window

Timeline

HOME VIDEO EDITING ▲
Adobe's home video edition of their Pro software is an affordable option for Windows users. Because it is aimed at the home market, it has a lot of cheesy effects and transitions.

CHECK THESE OUT

www.apple.com Final Cut Express, Final Cut Pro, and iMovie

www.adobe.com/motion
Premiere and Adobe Video Collection

www.avid.com The full range of Avid software, including Avid DV Free (Mac and Win)

In the Blink of an Eye
Walter Murch (Silman-James Press (2nd ed.), 2001

The Technique of Film Editing Karl Reisz and Gavin Miller (Focal Press, (2nd ed.), 1995)

First Cut: Conversations with Film Editors Gabriella Oldham (University of California Press, 1995)

The Conversations: Walter Murch and the Art of Editing Film Michael Ondaatje (Knopf, 2002)

Clips are stored here.

Preview windows.

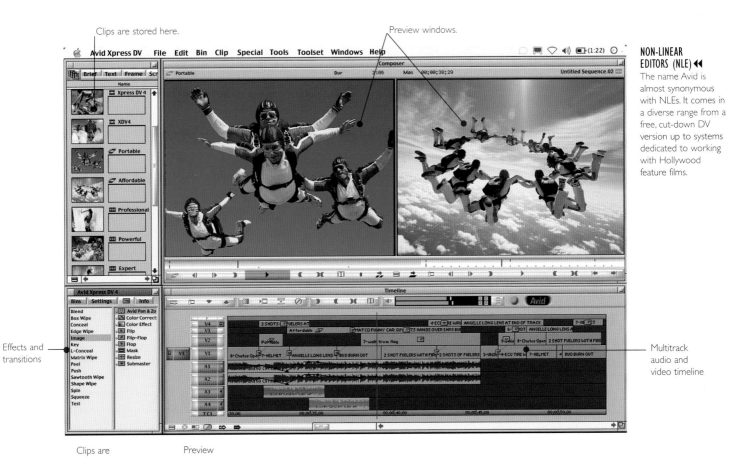

The name Avid is almost synonymous with NLEs. It comes in a diverse range from a free, cut-down DV version up to systems dedicated to working with Hollywood feature films.

Effects and transitions

Multitrack audio and video timeline

Clips are stored here.

Preview windows

BEST IN THE BUSINESS ◀◀

Adobe's flagship editing software is Windows only and represents great value as part of the Video Bundle. It has been around for a long time and has a dedicated following. It is easier to use than Avid and integrates with the rest of the Adobe range of software.

DON'T FADE AWAY

Editing software come with many different transitions and effects built in. There is always a temptation to use them—because they are there—but they may not be the best things for your movie. All the tricksy transitions should definitely be avoided and even subtler ones, such as dissolves, should be used sparingly and with discretion. Filters are not all for special effects; they also include things like color correction and balance, although a professional broadcast monitor is really needed to do this successfully. There are also third-party filters that can facilitate a lot of editing effects jobs, such as creating film looks or adding "scratches."

Although these effects can improve the look of your movie, if they are not used carefully they will make it look amateurish, and they will never make a badly scripted, shot, or edited film look good.

Multitrack audio and video timeline

SPECIAL EFFECTS

WITH SO MANY FILMS FILLED WITH CGI SPECIAL EFFECTS (SFX) ON RELEASE, IT CAN BE VERY TEMPTING FOR LOW-BUDGET FILMMAKERS TO WANT TO ADD SOME TO THEIR FILMS. TECHNOLOGICALLY, EFFECTS HAVE COME A LONG WAY FROM RAY HARRYHAUSEN'S HAND-BUILT, STOP-MOTION PUPPETS, SHOT FRAME BY FRAME IN FRONT OF A BACK-PROJECTED FILM IN HIS GARAGE.

- ▸▸ CGI effects
- ▸▸ Useful software
- ▸▸ Filters and other effects

STOP-MOTION ANIMATION ▼
Stop-motion animation using models was the primary method of special effects, before the advent of CGI. The detail in Ray Harryhausen's monsters is still impressive, even by today's standards.

With the incredible processing power of home computers and the low cost of the necessary software, there really is not a lot to stop filmmakers from trying to emulate ILM's efforts, not even pride or good taste. Yet with all the expertise that Hollywood studios can buy, they don't always achieve convincing results. Although Harryhausen's animations may not match modern CGI for realism, in terms of sheer craftsmanship he remains incomparable.

Modern special effects still use the same basic principle, animation mixed with live action, but instead of it being done frame by frame, it is now composited together on a computer. Horror, fantasy, and sci-fi, the main users of SFX, also happen to be very popular genres with low-budget moviemakers.

To make the most of CGI you need to start with a good 3D modeler and animator. The right talent will be able to produce stunning animation even with budget-priced software. Try to keep the animation simple and restricted to non-organic objects—spacecraft, robots, or buildings—so there is less chance of it looking unrealistic. Keep your use of CGI to a minimum, or use it where it doesn't have to be integrated with the live-action footage.

If you want to put actors into a scene created with 3D animations, you have to shoot them on a chroma key (blue screen or green screen) background. For best results, you need to shoot on at least 16mm film or one of the high-resolution digital formats that doesn't employ high compression. As well as a good camera, you will need either lots of blue or green chroma key paint or a backdrop cloth in the appropriate color. It is best to use a large studio space where there is plenty of room in which to set up the backgrounds and light them properly—you need to use strong, even lighting that doesn't cast shadows. The foreground action has to be lit to match the CGI elements. Filming in a large studio makes it possible to separate the background and foreground lighting, and it provides enough space to shoot with a longer lens that will both bring the background closer and throw it out of focus.

Going the other way, dropping 3D CGI characters into the live-action footage, you can create alpha masks that will be exported with the character to isolate it from its background. The CGI footage and the chroma key footage are combined using compositing software such as Adobe After Effects, Discreet Combustion, or Apple Shake. Most editing programs, such as Final Cut and Premiere, can

also handle chroma keying, although compositing software will give you more complex tools for 2D and 3D effects.

SCREEN PAINT

Apart from straightforward chroma key/CGI, all manner of effects can be achieved using filters or other effects programs. These are usually the preserve of pop videos or dream sequences and can easily stray toward the cheesy if not used with discretion. Using image-altering effects to compensate for bad shooting does not work. However, if you decide that your story needs the actors to turn into cartoon characters, or fall into the world of a Van Gogh painting, or an early silent movie, these effects are quite easily achievable, given the right software.

Not all effects have to be spectacular or fantastic. There are also little things that you might need to add to your film to give a touch of realism, such as a sign placed on a shop window, or the flash from the end of a prop gun when it is fired.

Although almost every feature film has some sort of post-production special effect, and some comprise only special effects, it is far more important to concentrate on producing a good story with believable characters than to try to emulate Hollywood. If using SFX is necessary to tell or enhance the story, do it sparingly, but remember that the breakthrough films of most independent directors were simple narratives, well told.

EFFECTIVE USE OF GREEN SCREEN ▲
The secret to getting good results with green screen is lighting and the positioning of the camera, actors, and backdrop.

GREEN SCREEN ▼
Green screen is not just the preserve of Hollywood blockbusters. It lets low-budget filmmakers create huge set pieces without the need of a construction crew and massive sound stage. In his homage to sci-fi B-movies, director Simon Davison shot his actors against green screens, then added backgrounds that were either 3D CGI created on computer, or cardboard models. These were all comped together using After Effects on a standard desktop computer (see www.captaineager.com).

KEEP EXPERIMENTING ◀
Create composite images through a 3D space.

COMPOSITING SOFTWARE ▼
Create a biker gang from a lone motorcyclist.

CREATING "ARTISTIC" EFFECTS ▼
Studio Artist is a Mac-only program designed primarily for giving "artistic" effects to photos, but it will also work with QuickTime movies. All effects are customizable and can be batch processed. Depending on the effect, they can take a long time to render, but for something different this program is worth a look.

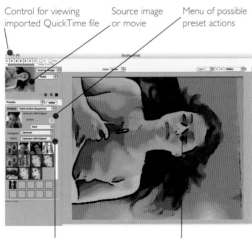

Control for viewing imported QuickTime file

Source image or movie

Menu of possible preset actions

Menus of preset styles: Styles can be customized under these menus.

Preview of rendered frame

SPECIAL EFFECTS

TITLES AND CREDITS

TITLES ARE AN IMPORTANT PART OF YOUR FILM. NOT ONLY WILL THEY IMPART NECESSARY INFORMATION TO THE VIEWER, THEY WILL ALSO HELP TO SET THE MOOD BEFORE THE NARRATIVE STARTS TO UNFOLD.

- ▸▸ Design
- ▸▸ Effects and software
- ▸▸ Thank yous!

RIGHT TYPE ⬇
Choosing an appropriate typeface will help to convey the mood of a film.

This doesn't always have to be the case, and the simplest static letters can work, but putting in that little bit of extra effort will demonstrate a professional attitude to the whole filmmaking process.

To create dynamic titles, you need to start considering their design as early as possible so that they can become part of the look of the production and promotion package (see pages 126–127).

TYPE CAST

The best place to start is with the selection of a typeface. Try to avoid the generic faces that come with your computer. Times Roman is a classic and, used discreetly, can look impressive, but from the thousands of typefaces available, you should be able to select something that exemplifies your movie's story or theme. If graphic design isn't one of your strengths, find someone who has a good eye for it and get them on the team, because you are going to need their skills throughout the production.

Once you have chosen a typeface or two (keep it simple), you and/or the designer can start working on concept ideas for titles and other material, such as

DYNAMIC TITLES ⬇
Apple LiveType is a simple way of producing dynamic, animated titles, when used with discretion.

posters. Because short films are just that, short, you need to keep the titles brief and possibly integrate them into the film itself—sometimes called TV titles. Chances are you won't have well-known actors, so you don't need to start with their names. Credits are best left to the end and made as concise as possible.

E MOTION

Most editing software comes with title/credit creation functions that cater to most needs. They usually have a range of pre-set effects that can be customized, but more often than not, these have a generic look that

The Serpent & The Apple

BEMBO ▲

The Seventh Circle

WILHELM KLINGSPOR GOTISCH ▲

MENACE

HELVETICA NEUE ▲

Kiss Chase

MISTER FRISKY ▲

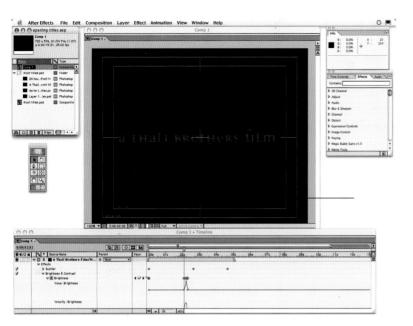

TITLES SOFTWARE ▲

Adobe After Effects is a compositing and special effects program that can also be used for creating unique titles for your film. After Effects can even integrate type into the movie in a 3D plane. It is a powerful and complex program that should be in any serious post-production suite, but don't buy it just for doing titles.

lacks the spark of originality. To create something unique you will need to use dedicated software such as Adobe After Effects or Discreet Combustion. Not exactly low-budget items, they are very powerful and versatile. Users of Apple's Final Cut editing programs get LiveType included in the package. This will create dynamic, animated type for use with the editing software, as will Motion, another motion-graphics editor from Apple.

Another all-around tool, Macromedia Flash is not cheap, but it is capable of producing everything from animated type to Web sites and interactive content. One of Flash's advantages is its small file sizes, for use on Web sites, but the .swf format will also integrate with video-editing software. For quick, inexpensive text effects, Wildform's WildFX Pro is a perfect solution, although some of the effects are a bit cheesy.

Not all film titles have to be computer generated. Invention is what low-budget moviemaking is all about: Use stop-motion animation techniques and collage; draw titles by hand and film them, or use a scanner and import the image files; or film the title written, painted, or printed onto a surface and integrate it into the scene. Whatever technique you choose to use, remember the maxim of good design: "Less is more."

CREDITS WHERE CREDIT'S DUE

The closing credits, when most people leave the theater, are mainly for the benefit of those whose names appear there. It is therefore important to include everyone who worked on or appeared in the movie, and to credit them properly. If they are working for nothing to gain experience, having their name at the end of the movie will help them to get more work. You will also need to thank everyone who donated services or locations, and include copyright and disclaimer information. Whatever style you use (rolling or static) the credits need to be on screen long enough to be read, but not so long that they impinge on the running time.

Given the general public's aversion to watching credits, filmmakers have tried enhancing them with outtakes (examples include the movies of Jackie Chan and Pixar). Others have put additional scenes after the credits, while some use a popular tune (see pages 98–99 for why you won't be doing this). Despite all these efforts, Joe Public still won't read the credits. The important thing is that they are there, and it is to be hoped that they will be read by the right people.

CHECK THESE OUT

Catch Me If You Can
(Dir. Steven Spielberg)

Conspiracy Theory
(Dir. Richard Donner)

eXisTenz (Dir. David Cronenberg)

Ghost in the Shell
(Anime, Dir. Mamoru Oshî)

Naked Lunch
(Dir. David Cronenberg)

 www.adobe.com/products/
aftereffects/main.html
AfterEffects

www.apple.com LiveType and Motion

www.discreet.com/combustion

www.macromedia.com Flash

Free typefaces
www.acidfonts.com
www.chank.com
www.fonthead.com
www.girlswhowear
glasses.com
www.houseind.com
www.larabiefonts.com

SOUND

THE IMPORTANCE OF SOUND HAS BEEN COVERED ON PAGES 72–75, BUT IT IS DURING POST-PRODUCTION THAT YOU CAN REALLY ELEVATE IT TO NEW REALMS. **N**O MATTER HOW HARD YOU TRY, EVEN ARMED WITH THE BEST EQUIPMENT IN THE WORLD, YOU ARE GOING TO MISS SOME OF THE AMBIENT SOUNDS YOU WANT AND GET SOME YOU DEFINITELY DON'T WANT. **S**O HOW DO YOU RESOLVE THIS?

▶▶ Hire an expert

▶▶ Editing and adding sound

▶▶ The dialogue track

SOUND ADVICE

One of the best things you can do is find yourself a good studio-based audio person. These are usually people who like playing around with audio waveforms on computers. Alternatively, find a technology-savvy musician, who comes with the bonus of being able to help compose the soundtrack. Whoever you choose, getting the optimum final sound is vital to your movie's presentation.

FOLEY AND SOUND EFFECTS

All your dialogue and wild-track recordings from the shoot should already be digitized and stored on the computer, either in your editing software or in a separate sound-editing program, such as ProTools. Depending on your software, you should allocate a separate track for each sound. An affordable video editor, such as Apple Final Cut Express, allows 99 audio tracks, and although it doesn't have the same level of control that the Pro version or Adobe Premiere offers, it is more than capable of producing a well-balanced, in-sync soundtrack. For a more complex sound mix, try a dedicated audio program such as ProTools or MOTU Digital Performer. These are music-recording/mixing programs, incorporating film-scoring facilities, favored by professional musicians. They are sophisticated and require an experienced user, but the results are excellent.

Any sounds that weren't captured during the shoot are added at the post-production stage. Work on sounds that need enhancing—footsteps, doors creaking, and so on—is usually done by foley artists. They create and record all manner of sounds and noises in a studio using their own favored props.

Hiring a good foley artist is going to be expensive, so you may have to settle for the cheaper option of pre-recorded sound effects. These are available on CDs or as downloads from Web sites, and the quality varies. Free downloads are available, but you get what you pay for. Commercial sites offer superior search facilities and previews, so you can be sure of exactly what you are acquiring. There are pitfalls in buying

DUBBING ▶▶

Sometimes the dialogue is not very clear during the shoot and must be re-recorded in a studio, preferably using the same recording equipment used during the shoot.

POPULAR SOUNDS

Hundreds of pre-recorded sound effects are available on Web sites or on CDs. These are some of the most popular and useful:

Gun shots

Creaking doors

Screeching tires

Car engine

Breaking glass

Footsteps

Explosions

Trains

Water drops/running water

Wind

Crying baby

Telephone (dialing, ringing, engaged)

Slamming doors

Sirens

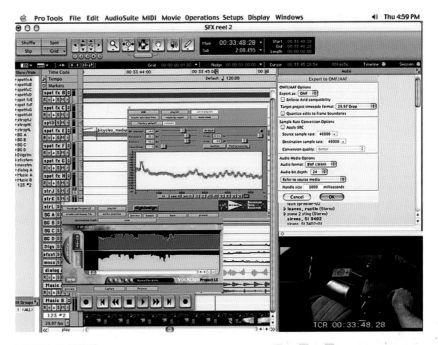

PROTOOLS DV TOOLKIT

DigiDesign ProTools is one of the industry's standard sound tools, which comes with a plug-in module for working with Digital Video.

CDs: you don't know what you are getting in advance, and you have to pay for a disc full of sounds you don't need, for the sake of one effect. This makes downloading individual sounds an attractive option.

ADR AND VOICEOVER

What happens when something goes wrong with the all-important dialogue track? Providing the visuals are okay, you can simply re-record the actors in a recording studio, or any place you can keep soundproof. Known as ADR (automatic dialogue replacement), it isn't going to be quite as automatic as it would be in a professional studio, but it is possible. Apart from a place to record, you will need a television or screen for the actors to watch, to get the lip-sync correct, and headphones so that they can try to match the original feeling. It is then just a

matter of recording onto DAT, HD recorder, or straight into a computer. You can change dialogue, if necessary, by editing the visuals so the new lines are spoken off-screen, providing you shot enough coverage in the first place. Tweak the freshly recorded voices using filters to match them to the rest of the scene. Any voiceovers are done in the same way and mixed into the soundtrack.

MIX AND MATCH

On feature films, sound engineers use huge multitrack mixing desks and the highest quality monitor speakers to ensure that the audio is well-balanced and what needs to be heard is audible. While you may only have access to a software mixer, you should make sure that you have good speakers, or at least top-quality headphones, that will allow you to hear the full dynamic range of the sounds; once you start incorporating music, this will be even more important.

CHECK THESE OUT

 www.bias-inc.com Peak and Deck sound-recording/editing software

www.motu.com Digital Performer recording and sequencing software

www.protools.com ProTools highly respected sound-editing software, integrates with Avid Xpress Pro editing software

www.digidesign.com/ptfree A free version of Pro Tools for Windows and Macs running System 9 (will not work with OSX or in Classic mode)

Sound-effects libraries:

www.sonymediasoftware.com/default.asp

www.powerfx.com

www.sound-effects-library.com

www.soundoftheweb.net

MUSIC

ONCE YOU HAVE ALL THE DIALOGUE AND SOUND EFFECTS IN PLACE, YOU WILL PROBABLY WANT TO ADD MUSIC. OF COURSE, YOU SHOULD HAVE BROUGHT THE SCORE COMPOSER ON BOARD AT THE PRE-PRODUCTION STAGE TO GIVE HIM OR HER A CHANCE TO START WORKING ON THEMES AND MOTIFS FOR THE MOVIE.

▶ Copyright

▶ Enhancing mood

▶ Sound mixing

You are probably wondering where you are going to find a composer for an original soundtrack and how you are going to pay them, when it would be easier just to use something from your CD collection.

As you must no doubt be aware, the music industry (not necessarily the musicians) is very strict on the enforcement of its rights. If you use an existing track, you will have to pay for it, and you will also have to deal with all sorts of contracts. If you are going to use music, DO NOT USE EXISTING MUSIC, unless it is royalty-free and properly licensed. There is a lot of library music available, of varying quality and price, but whether it exactly fits your film can be a matter of luck.

KNOWING THE SCORE

Music in film helps to establish themes or to create mood. The style of the music will depend on the type of film and the idea you are trying to convey. It will also be influenced by your taste, and by your budget. Whatever genre of music you want to use, it is best to make sure that it is original. If you are not a musician, or don't know one, or, worse, know one who isn't very good but insists on helping, what can you do? If you use any of Apple's video-editing software (Final Cut Pro, or Express, or even iMovie), you will also have access to music software designed for people not very adept with musical instruments. GarageBand and Soundtrack use prerecorded loops of real musical instruments that can be sequenced and layered to create a rich, original soundtrack. The Soundtrack program is designed for use with video so that all the sound can be cued properly.

CHECK THESE OUT

Complete Guide to Film Scoring Richard Davis (Berklee Press Publications, 2000)

From Score to Screen Sonny Kompanek (Schirmer Trade Books, 2004)

On Track: A Guide to Contemporary Film Scoring Fred Karlin, Rayburn Wright (Routledge (2nd ed.), 2004)

The Reel World: Scoring for Pictures Jeff Rona (Backbeat Books, 2000)

www.adobe.com/products/audition Audition audio software to integrate with Premiere for Windows

www.apple.com/ilife/garageband GarageBand, Soundtrack, and Logic audio software

www.bias-inc.com Peak and Deck sound-recording and editing software

www.groovemaker.com Loop editor for Windows and Mac

www.sonymedia.com/products SoundForge and other audio programs

www.motu.com Digital Performer recording and sequencing software

www.steinberg.de Cubase and Nuendo software for music and media production

These programs cannot fully replace a talented composer who is trained to understand how to evoke emotions through music, but they will do a more than satisfactory job.

Being able to create the music is not enough; to get maximum impact it is vital to know when and where to use it. Study a wide range of films to learn what works best in particular situations. The most successful scores are those you don't notice but that still manage to enhance the visuals or the mood. In fact, we have become so used to music in films (as in our everyday lives with the ubiquity of portable music players) that its absence becomes unsettling—something worth considering when designing the soundtrack.

Once your musical score is completed, it has to be mixed in with the rest of the sound. Stereo sound is standard, and for early films this should be more than sufficient for most viewing situations. If you really want to enhance the aural experience with surround sound (5.1), you will have to use specialized software such as Bias Deck, ProTools, Nuendo, or Audition. Some of these are quite affordable, and if they are used properly, they will certainly give your film a professional sound.

SURROUND SOUND ▶▶

With home entertainment centers being commonplace, incorporating surround sound into your finished movie will give it that extra professional touch. Software, such as DigiDesign ProTools, is needed to get the sounds in the correct channels.

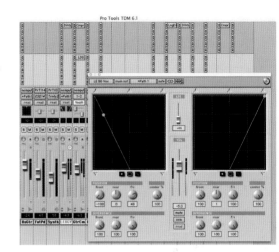

SOUND LOOPS ▼

Apple's Soundtrack is one of a number of programs that let non-musicians create their own musical scores using pre-recorded loops of instruments and sound effects. Included as part of the Final Cut editing package, it is designed to work precisely with movies and provides an almost foolproof way of creating an original soundtrack without copyright or royalties issues.

Sound loops are divided into categories to make searching easier. A loop can appear in more than one category.

Video is previewed in this window. A QuickTime file is required. Final Cut exports files specifically for Soundtrack with cuing markers embedded.

Audio markers inserted in Final Cut as a guide for the music.

Timeline, showing frames from the movie where the markers were inserted.

Timer and playback controls.

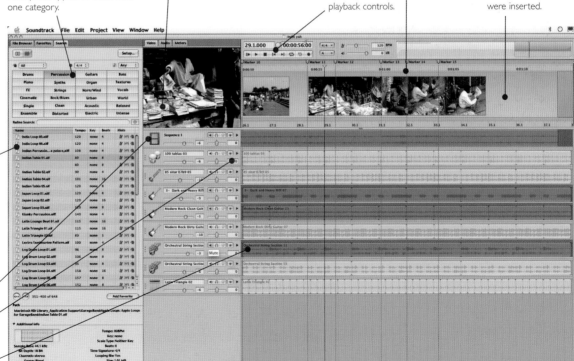

Sound loops appear in an alphabetical list and can be previewed by clicking on them. Information about the loop is shown alongside the name and at the bottom of the list.

The film's recorded dialogue track.

Loops are dragged from the list, on the left, onto a layer of the timeline. Its name and controls appear in the column to the left.

The greyed-out tracks have been muted (switched off).

POST-PRODUCTION

STRAIGHT TO VIDEO?

IDEALLY, THE FINAL OUTPUT MEDIUM WILL HAVE BEEN THOUGHT ABOUT DURING THE PRE-PRODUCTION STAGE WHEN THE SHOOTING MEDIUM WAS BEING SELECTED. THE DECISION WILL BE INFLUENCED BY WHAT YOU INTEND TO DO WITH THE MOVIE ONCE IT IS FINISHED. ARE YOU AIMING FOR THE FESTIVAL CIRCUIT? TV? DVD? INTERNET?

- ▸▸ Distribution decisions
- ▸▸ Digital viewing
- ▸▸ Advantages for the low-budget filmmaker

More about these options is covered in the following pages, but the final edit has to be taken off the computer and put into a format for distribution and viewing.

If you've shot on film (16mm), then you may want to keep it on film. This means translating your digital edit to the original film negatives. It also means getting prints made from the final-cut negatives so it can be projected. While 16mm projectors are still in use, most cinemas only have 35mm projectors. This means that if you want to show a film at a festival, you will have to get a 35mm blow-up from the 16mm negative, and this is not cheap. Prints are charged by the foot, so a ten-minute film is not going to cost as much as a feature film—but then again the distributor will pay the cost of prints for a cinema-released feature. When it comes to showing shorts at festivals, the cost lies with the filmmaker. Most festivals barely break even financially, so they are unable to pay for prints.

DIGITAL PROJECTOR ▲
With more films being made digitally, greater numbers of movie theaters are investing in digital cameras. Relatively inexpensive consumer projectors mean that small venues, such as clubs, can now easily show digital shorts.

FESTIVAL FORMATS ▸▸
If you have limited resources, withoutabox.com lets you search for festivals that accept specific formats so you don't have to get your movie converted before submitting it.

DIGITAL PROJECTION

Until recently, a movie shot digitally would have to be converted to film for distribution, as did all the CGI animations. This is a very expensive process that can end up costing more than shooting on film in the first place. More and more studio-backed feature films are being shot digitally, so cinemas are slowly installing digital projectors. With large cinemas being divided into multiplexes of smaller theaters, they no longer need very powerful equipment to project a good image on the screen. The proliferation of small screens is also opening up opportunities for independent

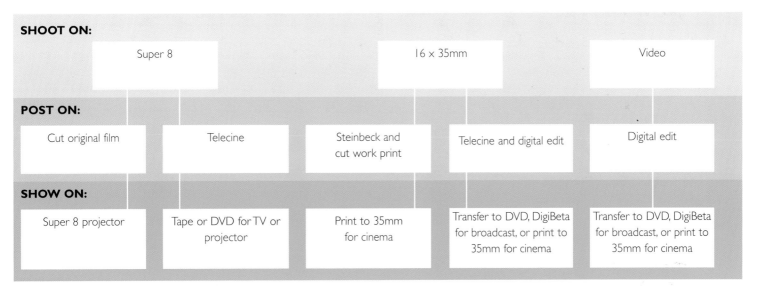

SHOOT ON:				
Super 8		16 x 35mm		Video
POST ON:				
Cut original film	Telecine	Steinbeck and cut work print	Telecine and digital edit	Digital edit
SHOW ON:				
Super 8 projector	Tape or DVD for TV or projector	Print to 35mm for cinema	Transfer to DVD, DigiBeta for broadcast, or print to 35mm for cinema	Transfer to DVD, DigiBeta for broadcast, or print to 35mm for cinema

PATHS TO GLORY ▲

How you get to show your film will be dictated by your choice of media and format. This chart shows the main options for the most popular formats used by independent filmmakers.

moviemakers to find spaces to show their movies, often using relatively inexpensive digital projectors similar to those designed for domestic and office use.

Most festivals now use these systems, because they realize that the majority of up-and-coming moviemakers are taking advantage of the low cost of shooting digitally. Filmmakers are using the money saved on film stock either to increase production values, or simply as an opportunity to make a movie that would previously have been impossible to contemplate financially.

Even if your movie was shot on film, and especially the smaller 16mm and Super 8 gauges, outputting to digital is certainly economically more viable, with duplication and distribution costs practically eliminated.

The popularity of the DVD format and its ever-decreasing costs have opened up new opportunities for independent filmmakers. Shooting digitally, there is very little degradation of image quality from what is captured on camera and what goes on the DVD. (Of course you have to remember the old computer maxim, GIGO—garbage in, garbage out.) This means it is possible for a filmmaker to produce a commercial-quality DVD on an inexpensive computer, assuming he or she has the technical and artistic skills. The work will look great on home televisions and even on larger screens using digital projectors.

BROADCAST

If you are aiming for television broadcast, you may need to look at supplying (and shooting) on professional formats, such as Betacam, Digibeta, or DVCAM, that have the correct resolution, but a well-shot miniDV will be accepted if the broadcaster wants the content. With the imminent move to high definition (HD) broadcasting, this will all change, but lower-budget HD solutions are already available, further improving your chances of producing broadcast-quality material.

In the short term and for the foreseeable future, digital distribution and viewing is to the advantage of low-budget independent filmmakers, whether for home entertainment DVD, broadcast, or digital projection in cinemas. Finding a market for your short film is another matter.

PROJECTS

This section provides a collection of projects, ideas, and case studies to inspire
you to put the book away and get shooting.

The beauty of the short format is that it allows you to make any type of
film, free from the constraints imposed by features and television shows.
Short films can run for anything between 30 seconds and 30 minutes,
although some lengths are more commercially viable than others, and all the
projects here run to a maximum of 15 minutes.

Most of the projects are not straightforward narrative films. They represent
a variety of genres and styles, including animation and formats without actors.
There is also advice on some well-established competition formats that will
test your imagination and ingenuity to their limits.

Not all the projects are based on digital video either. All film formats
(Super 8, 16mm, and 35mm) are also included, as well as non-camera
methods. Explore all the projects and even mix them together. Let serendipity
be your guide. The important thing is to start making movies and discover
what you can create. Who knows when your name will appear on the list of
Academy Award nominations?

15-SECOND FILM

IN THE TIME IT TAKES THE AVERAGE PERSON TO READ THE TITLE AND THIS SENTENCE, YOU WILL HAVE TOLD YOUR STORY AND THE FILM WILL BE OVER. COUNT THE SECONDS ON YOUR WATCH. DESPITE THE BREVITY, THERE ARE TELEVISION COMMERCIALS THAT TAKE THAT MUCH (OR THAT LITTLE) TIME TO SELL YOU AN ENTIRE LIFESTYLE CONCEPT.

▶▶ Keep it simple

▶▶ Straight to the punch line

▶▶ An exercise in editing

Admittedly, the 15-second commercial is an ‘edited version of a longer spot, usually inserted at the end of a commercial break to reinforce the message, so it does not have to convey a complete idea. But what about a stand-alone, ultra-short movie? What is its purpose?

The idea was dreamed up by advertising and marketing people, to whom the 15-second concept was already familiar, as a way of promoting the new generation of video cell phones. The limit was set partly because of the restrictions of the technology, and partly as a challenge to filmmakers. Outside of the original Nokia competition, there is an increasing demand for content from the phone networks as they try to offer more variety to customers.

LITTLE IDEAS

Like all films, a 15-second opus needs an idea; in fact, the whole film will be the expression of that basic idea, so the simpler it is, the better. There is no time for complex character development or establishing a backstory. You have to set up the concept and get straight to the punch line, which probably represents one of the best devices to make it entertaining. In this type of movie, the punch line provides the surprise, and sometimes the shock, ending. Try not to make it too gruesome, upsetting, or offending to viewers. It is always better to use humor, even if it is a bit sinister. You must ensure that the idea is resolved, avoiding the impression of incompletion. If you are using actors, find people who have very expressive faces.

ASSIGNMENT

AIM:
✗ Create a 15-second movie, with or without sound, to show on a cell phone.

CREW:
✗ Director
✗ Camera operator
✗ Editor

EQUIPMENT:
✗ MiniDV or DV camera

READY TO ROLL ▲
The car set up for the shoot. The black cloth was used to prevent reflections in the car's windscreen. The white reflector was used to bounce the light taken away by the black sheet back into the car.

HAVE I PASSED?

INT. CAR – DAY
A nervous STUDENT DRIVER sits beside a weary EXAMINER.
EXAMINER(consulting clipboard)
Parallel parking, turns, emergency stop. All excellent.

STUDENT DRIVER
So?

1   2

QUICK SHOTS

Once you have your basic idea, you have to shoot it. Even if you intend it to be used only for cell phone content, it is still best shot on at least a miniDV camera. Don't try to shoot using the camera in the phone. It is much easier to reduce the resolution of a movie than to increase what wasn't there in the first place. Even though the final movie will be only 15 seconds long, you need to make sure you shoot enough footage. The shooting ratio will be much greater than it would be for, say, a feature, or even for a ten-minute short.

Of course, you don't have to create a complex, multiple-shot extravaganza. There is nothing to stop you from doing it all in a single take, if the idea works—and in 15 seconds, there is no reason it shouldn't.

SHAVING CUTS

The longest part of the project will be the editing. Your first rough cut could be anywhere from 30 to 60 seconds. Now you have to start shaving away the seconds, and making decisions about how much and which parts of the shot best convey the idea. The only way to do this is to keep playing it over and over until it reduces to the required length. As a learning exercise, editing a 15-second film will teach you a lot about the economy of shot usage, and this will be invaluable when you come to make longer short films.

If you can make a 15-second film successfully, anything longer should be just that much easier.

HAVE I PASSED? – SHOT LIST

	SECONDS
Black, cut to	
"HAVE I PASSED" in large font on screen, single line, cut to...	3
CU: A pen scribbles on a pad, on a page headed Driving Exam, checking boxes. Another sheet is being held up. MUSIC plays in the background. The Examiner mumbles to herself, "emergency stop," etc.	2
MID: (Behind Student, high, on Examiner, framed by Student seat), lowers sheet. Concludes "all fine."	3
MID: (Behind Examiner, high, on Student, framed by Examiner seat), Student leaning into window, hand on wheel asks "So?", confident.	2
BACK ON EXAMINER who turns off music, shows clipboard. Carry "But you still haven't passed" over into, and match action into...	3
LOW: (From Examiner seat, clipboard into shot top right, Student on right too), Student looks down, clipboard flies up. Looks down from clipboard briefly on noise of door shutting.	3
WIDE: Over the car, Examiner turns from car with raised brows, taking deep breath, walks off.	2
Credits 1	2.5
Credits 2	2.5

EXAMINER
But you still haven't passed.

The Examiner shifts to climb out, placing clipboard and pen on the dash. The clipboard and pen fly upward.

EXT. CAR – CONTINUOUS
The Examiner clambers out of the UPSIDE-DOWN car – Watched by the frustrated Student Driver. And an incredulous PASSER-BY.

3   4   5

10-MINUTE DOCUMENTARY

THERE HAS BEEN A SIGNIFICANT RISE IN THE POPULARITY OF THE DOCUMENTARY IN RECENT
YEARS, THANKS IN PART TO MICHAEL MOORE AND HIS INTERNATIONAL SUCCESSES.

▶▶ Share your passions

▶▶ The right equipment

▶▶ Shoot everything;
   edit later

ASSIGNMENT

AIM:
✗ Produce a ten-minute documentary on a subject of your choice using digital video.

CREW:
✗ Director
✗ Camera operator
✗ Sound recorder

EQUIPMENT:
✗ Digital video camera
✗ Microphone
✗ Camera support

Anti-establishment and political documentary features were big in 2004, and they overshadowed the thousands of other documentaries shot throughout that and every other year. Television still shows a lot of non-fiction programs that aren't "reality" or game shows. Nature and wildlife programs, travel programs, educational shows—the list is endless, and if you want your film to be on that list, you need a subject you are passionate about and want to share with others.

Most television programming is divided into 30- and 60-minute slots, but some broadcasters have five- and ten-minute slots they want to fill, often with something quirky that isn't a narrative. These short spots need to be informative, entertaining, and visually captivating, offering a little-seen window on the world.

If this sort of filmmaking appeals to you, and you want to be broadcast, you have to use the right equipment. Broadcast quality usually means shooting on the expensive DigiBeta format, but the arrival of HDV has opened up new possibilities for the low-budget filmmaker, especially for documentaries. At a stretch, it is possible to shoot on miniDV or DVCAM, although the better the quality of the image, the better the chances of it being aired.

Digital video, in any of its flavors, is a great boon to the documentary filmmaker. Documentaries usually require hours of footage that have to be whittled down to something succinct, and the low cost of tape makes this possible. It is also easier to log and edit. The cameras are lighter and less intrusive, making the whole shoot easier.

Equipment aside, as with any movie, it is content that is most important. How you approach, interpret,

POSSIBLE SUBJECTS

Your documentary will be that much more interesting if the subject is something you are passionate about. Here are some ideas to get you thinking:

1 Extreme sports: skateboarding, BMX riding, surfing, hang-gliding...

2 Preparing a traditional meal

3 Commuting on public transportation

4 Making a comic book

5 Making articles of clothing, for example, a handmade suit

6 Body piercing

7 Obsessive collecting

8 A Day in the Life of a Dollar Bill

SHOOT SCRIPT ▶▶

How much of your documentary you script beforehand will depend on the type of film you are making. Because it is being shot from life, there is very little that can be pre-planned, although rough outlines can be drawn up and, if interviews are to be included, some questions prepared. A voiceover script would be written once everything has been edited. The script here, for a short doc about a snowboarder, is a pre-shoot one, with an outline and some questions.

POSITIONING ▲

Finding the best position for a shot can mean being positioned well away from your subject. Walkie-talkies are an invaluable way to stay in contact. There are rarely chances for a retake, so you don't want the subject moving before the camera is ready. It takes a lot of organization to make it look spontaneous.

The Whites of their Ice *(working title)*
Brad Neve: Extreme Snowboarder *(subtitle)*
Running time: *10–15 minutes*

Brad is best known for his almost vertical drops in isolated backcountry powder snow. Because we have no helicopters, positioning will be important to get the best action shots.

We need at least two cameras for each drop. These will be difficult shots but we need as many as possible during the week. At least one extreme telephoto lens will be needed.

We will also need lots of half pipe shots (using a very wide-angle lens).

Brad is also known for being a party animal and a prankster. One camera should follow him when he's not boarding. Keep it as non-invasive as possible, but he will probably play up to the camera. Try to get stuff of him relaxing too. Don't film any illegal activity as it won't be used, and it's better not to have it at all than to have to delete it.

Sample interview questions

● Why do you do it?

● Is it the fear element that gives you the rush?

● Do you scout out a place before you ride, or just go for it and hope for the best?

● Any safety precautions?

● Some people do a lot of mental and physical preparation before taking big drops, but you seem really relaxed. How do you prepare?

● Big wave surfers always talk about their awe and respect for the ocean. What is your attitude towards the mountains?

● What is the worst you've hurt yourself while snowboarding?

● Most people tend to specialize in one style, but you are known just as well for your pipe moves. Which do you prefer?

● You have not entered the pro circuit, yet you could give any of those guys a run for their money. How come you don't compete?

and present your subject is what matters. Although there is a certain unknown quantity to the shoot that comes from filming real life, you still need to start with a clear concept of what you want to achieve. This may change during, or after, the shoot, but without an original plan you will be, as it were, shooting in the dark.

For your first documentary, don't be too ambitious. Pick a subject you are passionate about. It doesn't have to be anything political; it could be an extreme sport, music, fishing, cooking, or trains. It's your enthusiasm for the topic that counts—and your ability to find a unique way of showing it.

For example, do you like comics and know a comic-book artist? Why not film the creation of a page from concept to sketches to inks and colors? Film the studio, with different shots of the drawing process and coloring techniques. Interview the artist and film him or her doing something other than drawing. Try to incorporate some of the comic into the film's narrative. Shoot every stage of drawing and shoot lots, and from as many different angles as possible. Get close-ups of hands, face, eyes, mouth. Shoot over the shoulder, long shots, medium shots. Remember that tape is cheap and you rarely get a second chance to go back and shoot again. Sometimes you can mock up insert shots, especially with interviews, but in this example, reshooting a drawing, while not impossible, is best avoided—and remember continuity.

Editing all the footage together needs a slightly different approach from the standard narrative movie because faster cuts can be used without worrying about disturbing the story's flow. It can be tied much more closely to the soundtrack, and even cut to an existing (original) score. The important thing is to establish a good rhythm in the editing.

Of course, there is another type of documentary that can serve the novice filmmaker twofold—the behind-the-scenes-making-of-DVD-extras type. If you can find someone who is making a movie, offer to go and shoot all the behind-the-scenes stuff. Tell them you are learning about filmmaking and want to practice by making a documentary. Offer to share the results but make it clear there are no guarantees, if it is one of your first efforts. You will learn not only while you are shooting, but also from watching experienced filmmakers.

These are just a couple of suggestions but, as with any genre, you have to get out and do it.

SKILL ◀◀
For action sports, the cameraman needs to be able to follow focus accurately, and pan and tilt at the same time as holding a good composition. A good tripod and familiarity with the equipment are vital.

UP CLOSE AND PERSONAL ⬆
Documentaries invariably require the camera to get close to the action. Wide-angle lenses are important for this, as is some knowledge and experience of the subject, especially if there is some danger involved.

CHECK THESE OUT

www.docurama.com Distributes documentary films

www.fullframefest.org U.S. film festival for documentary filmmakers

www.escreeningroom.org A distribution channel for independent documentary films

Discovery Channel Excellent shorts used between main programs.

MUSIC VIDEO

THE MUSIC VIDEO, THE POP PROMO, WHATEVER YOU WANT TO CALL IT, IS AN IDEAL MEDIUM FOR ANY FILMMAKER TO EXPERIMENT WITH BECAUSE THERE ARE NO RULES AS SUCH. THERE ARE ALSO HUNDREDS OF BANDS AND PERFORMERS NEEDING SHORT FILMS TO PROMOTE THEIR SONGS.

- ▶▶ Finding a subject
- ▶▶ Selling the artist
- ▶▶ Which medium?

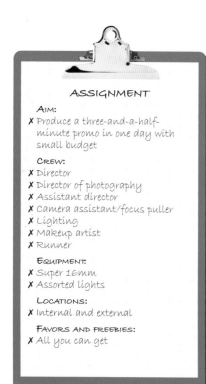

ASSIGNMENT

AIM:
✗ Produce a three-and-a-half-minute promo in one day with small budget

CREW:
✗ Director
✗ Director of photography
✗ Assistant director
✗ Camera assistant/focus puller
✗ Lighting
✗ Makeup artist
✗ Runner

EQUIPMENT:
✗ Super 16mm
✗ Assorted lights

LOCATIONS:
✗ Internal and external

FAVORS AND FREEBIES:
✗ All you can get

At the top end you can be dealing with budgets bigger than most independent features; at the bottom are the lo-no budget shoots in which you are more likely to be involved.

Because of the creative freedom that music video offers, there are just as many filmmakers looking for artists as there are musicians looking for filmmakers, so if you want to break into this field it won't hurt to do a little market research first. The best place to start is with yourself. What type of music do you like? What style or genre of films do you like or want to make? Do the two complement each other?

Go to see as many local bands performing as you can. Talk to the band or their manager to find out what their ambitions and prospects are. Let them know you are a filmmaker looking for a band to shoot, but don't be too quick to offer your services. Choose an artist or band that you want to film, and whose music and performance you like.

If you find a band with a recording contract, or one good enough to be signed, they are going to need a video. A band is generally expected to have a completed package before a record company will sign them. That means a finished EP or album and at least one video. By offering to work for a deferred payment, and by clever negotiation, you may be able to get yourself a good deal. Many bands don't realize that the cost of making their expensive video comes out of their advance/royalties and is not met by the record company. Approaching a band with this knowledge should help you to sell your services. If you give them a carefully budgeted schedule and explain that they will be paying for the video themselves, as the record company is only providing a

IN MAKEUP ▲
The makeup artist is often overlooked on the music video shoot, but is an essential member of the team—especially when working with female artists in close-up.

CREATING ATMOSPHERE ▲
A smoke machine is used here to give atmosphere to the nightclub setting.

REHEARSALS ▲
The DoP and the focus puller work together for a close-up shot using a long lens. The vocalist sings along to her recording for lip-synching at the post-production stage, but no live sound is being recorded on the shoot.

loan, you will immediately gain their confidence. After that, it is up to you to produce the goods.

What you shoot for the music video is something you'll have to discuss with the band. If you can approach them with an original concept, rather than letting them come up with an idea, it is going to be more enjoyable for you. The film you make is going to be very important to you. It will go on your showreel and your next job could depend on it.

Creating a story based around the song, or the mood it evokes, is often a good approach. However, making anything that is overly arty or conceptual could work against you. The film has to sell the band/artist as well as the song, so they will have to make an appearance in it somewhere. On the other hand, try to avoid a straight performance film; they can be a little dull after repeat viewing, even if record companies like this style for new artists. However, they are quick and easy to shoot, and in the end it is all about image and marketing the artist.

The arrival of the music DVD has opened a whole new range of opportunities for the music-video maker. Previously, only singles releases were turned into videos, but now whole albums are given the visual treatment. As nearly all music videos are destined for the small screen, you can shoot in almost any medium without having to resort to 35mm film. If you want to shoot film, 16mm/Super 16 is more than adequate. Even Super 8 is a possibility. Most semi-pro and pro DV cameras are more than adequate for the job, but better still are the new HDV cameras. On a lo-no budget route, DV is really your only option. With the right lighting and cameraman, the results will be perfect for its intended end use.

Try to make something that isn't going to date as fast as the music. Avoid excessive flashy special effects. The average viewer may be impressed but other filmmakers will instantly recognize that new software plug-in. Using bits of traditional animation might be more interesting.

Whatever you envisage and shoot, it has to fit with the music, not only in temperament but also in tempo. You should give great consideration to rhythm in any filmmaking project, especially at the editing stage, but it is the driving force behind a music video.

Whatever you want to do with the music video, be original but stay faithful to the music, and don't let yourself be ripped off.

CHECK THESE OUT

MTV or any other music channel

Directors Label DVD series from Palm Pictures Highlights the work of some of the best music video directors over the last decade

www.shootingpeople. org An online network of filmmakers

www.musicvideo insider.com An e-zine and online community for music video directors

www.mvwire.com An online resource for the music video industry with news, interviews, and educational content

RAIN STOPS PLAY ◄◄
Filming on a rooftop, overlooking the city lights, was delayed by rain and strong wind, but went ahead because of time constraints with the borrowed equipment and "volunteer" crew.

DOUBLE CHECKS BEFORE FILMING ◄◄
A good crew is invaluable during a shoot and even more so when using film; as film stock will be your greatest expense on this type of shoot, experienced operators make sure everything runs smoothly. Here the assistant director (AD) and assistant cameraman double-check the equipment before the shoot.

AND MORE REHEARSALS ◄◄
Most musicians are confident performers in front of audiences and cameras. In performance-based videos they will need minimal direction, but rehearsal before exposing film is still vital.

48-HOUR FILM

ONE OF THE BIGGEST HURDLES FACING NEW FILMMAKERS IS ACTUALLY GETTING STARTED. THERE IS ALWAYS SOMETHING PREVENTING THE MOVIE FROM BEING MADE—NO SCRIPT, NO CAMERA, NO ACTORS, NO IDEA, OR NO TIME. IN RESPONSE TO THIS DILEMMA, THE 48-HOUR FILM CHALLENGE WAS DEVISED, TO ENCOURAGE FILMMAKING WITHOUT EXCUSES.

▶▶ Take up the challenge

▶▶ Working with a team

▶▶ Planning your time

ASSIGNMENT

AIM:

✗ Produce a five-minute movie on digital video within 48 hours, without knowing the genre or title until the beginning of the time limit.

CREW:

✗ Director
✗ Camera operator
✗ Sound recorder
✗ Makeup artist

EQUIPMENT:

✗ Digital video camera
✗ Microphone
✗ Camera support
✗ Props

Like all good ideas there is some debate about who thought of it first, but versions appeared in the U.S., Canada, and the U.K., all around the same time.

The premise behind the challenge has regional variations but is basically the same: shoot a five-minute film on miniDV within 48 hours. Although this is a challenge in itself, there is an added factor that makes it all the more interesting: it can't be planned ahead because the title and genre are not given until the beginning of the time limit. In its simplest form, contestants select a genre and a title from a "hat," then go off and make their film. To complicate matters further, or simply to circumvent any possible pre-planning, additional elements are thrown into the mix, such as including a specific object, a certain location, or a designated line of dialogue. Another variation has

each team create a package containing a sound, a photograph, a location idea, and a prop. The packages are then mixed up and distributed among the other teams. Other restrictions include such things as limiting the size of the team, setting a minimum number of actors, and giving a specific running time for the finished movie. By setting a "no shorter than/no longer than" time limit, the competition becomes more egalitarian.

BE PREPARED

There is no sure-fire way to prepare for such an event as the parameters will be changed with each competition. However, some steps can be taken to make things run more smoothly, and they all hinge around your team.

REHEARSALS ▶▶

The film's genre is "war" and the title is *Busted*. The team decide, given their limited resources, to base the film on a children's game that involves boys playing hooky from school. To speed up the filming, it's also decided to have no dialogue, or if any is needed, to add it in at post-production, along with sound effects and music. Here, the director makes the boys rehearse some of the scripted scenes while he decides on angles and framing.

Making a short movie from start to finish in 48 hours is a very intense experience. Creative differences and lack of sleep can produce very volatile situations, so the most important thing is to have a clearly defined leader (not necessarily the director). There are two possible approaches to recruiting team members. One is to gather a team of professional or highly experienced specialists who don't know each other. Given that familiarity breeds contempt, by the time your team actually gets to know each other, the shoot will be over. Also, being specialists, they only need to be around to fulfill their appointed tasks. Finding such a team and convincing them to be part of such a folly, especially for a novice, will not be easy.

The alternative is to get a group of your friends, with whom you've been through thick and thin, just go for it, and have fun. If you approach it without taking it too seriously—that is, with no expectation of winning—it is still possible to create something worthwhile. As the leader, you may decide to take on a lot of the technical/creative roles yourself (directing, camera, editing) and leave your friends to act, hold booms, and make coffee.

Busted

Day – Int: Suburban home
ALEX is ready for school. His backpack is full as we see him disappear out the front door. His MOTHER comes down the stairs, calling out to the shutting door as she spies his English folder lying on the floor. She picks it up and opens the door.

Day – Ext: Suburban street
Alex's mother calls down the street after Alex to give him his folder. Alex runs back, kisses his mother, and runs down the street, disappearing around a corner.

Day – Ext: Another suburban street (cont.)
Alex throws the folder under a bush, out of sight, and continues his journey.

Day – Ext: Outside school gates (cont.)
Alex runs past the school gates and finds his friend, DAVID, waiting for him.

Day – Ext: Tree-covered park
From their backpacks the boys pull out camouflage jackets, balaclavas, and toy guns. They change from school uniform to army uniform. David faces a tree and starts counting to himself as Alex runs off into the woods. David pursues him. The boys play hunter and hunted all day until one of them is finally "killed."

Day – Ext: Suburban home
Alex arrives home as his mother is taking the garbage out. He is tired but greets his mother enthusiastically. As he goes toward the door his mother instinctively picks something from his hair. She looks at it and does a slow double-take as her son enters the house.

Fade out
Credits

DISCUSSING IDEAS ◀◀
Most of the action of the game is improvised, but in order for the director to know what to do with the camera, he runs through the young actors' ideas with them.

SAMPLE SCRIPT PAGE ▲
The action for this simple storyline is explained in a single script page.

Whatever the creative conditions of the challenge are, the process to be followed is the same as with any other short-film project, but compressed into a weekend. The pre-production will be long. Devising a story to fit the genre/title, props, etc., is always time-consuming, requiring brainstorming and openness to other people's ideas. It seems to be inevitable that if there is a genre your team particularly does not like, that will be the one you get. The story has to be devised within the limitations of your props, locations, and actors, whether these limitations are imposed by the organizers or by your team's dynamics.

STARTING TO FILM

Once a story has been fleshed out, start filming as soon as possible. There will not be a lot of time for rehearsals, so shoot right away; if you can get two cameras, so much the better. Film all the rehearsals, and keep an accurate shot log to make it easier to find the best takes when it comes to editing. The more you shoot, the better your choice will be. Get all the shots you need but don't spend too much time doing it, as you will need at least 12 hours to edit and add sound. You also need to factor in time for the unforeseen—such as equipment failure.

ADDING A SOUNDTRACK

Make your rough cut as quickly as possible to give your composer time to create the soundtrack. Musicians will often have a supply of musical motifs they can access—ideas they have been tinkering with but have never completed—and that can be easily adapted, especially if they are digital recordings. Once the final cut of the visuals has been made, the soundtrack can be adjusted to fit.

When your film is edited and the soundtrack is mixed and synched, it is just a matter of transferring it from your computer to the specified medium and returning to the place from which you started.

Completing one of these 48-hour challenges will probably change the way you approach filmmaking for a long time. Watching crews agonizing for hours over a 20-second shot will be just that, agonizing. If there is no organized 48-hour challenge in your area, you can still do it yourself, or with some friends.

READY OR NOT ◀◀
Several of the park scenes are shot "handheld" to give a war zone documentary feel, especially while the boys are chasing each other through the woods.

LOGGING ◀◀
With the 48-hour time constraint, logging every shot and clearly describing it makes the editor's job a lot easier. Knowing what was shot, where to find it, and whether it was any good saves precious hours that can be utilized for tightening the edit and keeping it under five minutes.

PAY-OFF SCENE ◀◀
The crucial pay-off scene is shot at the end of the first day, after the park shots. The opening scenes are shot on the following morning, to get the lighting right. The editor had already started assembling the other scenes, in anticipation of the arrival of the new footage, to make the final cut.

GENRES

Genres can be combined, for example, a Romantic-Horror-Western movie.

Comedy

Western

Romance

Horror

Mockumentary

Action/ Adventure

Musical

Mystery

Detective/Cop

Fantasy

Black Comedy

Documentary

Rites of Passage/ Teen

Superhero

Spy

Buddy Picture

European Art House

SciFi

Martial Arts/ Kung Fu

TITLES

Choose a title at random from the possibilities shown here.

Screening Process

Widowmaker

Mind the Gap

Conversion

Dead Cool

Dog Gone Afternoon

Job Huntin'

Original Thought

Interference

Capitol Punishment

Intercept

Night Flight

Seeing is Believing

Staff Only

Dead Letter

Justice League

Sleeping Standing

The Cure

Clan Destiny

Crisis

Panic

What Am I Doing Here?

Reservation

Conditions Apply

IDEA GENERATOR ◀◀

Planning your own 48-hour film project? On this page is a list of genres and titles to choose from.

CHECK THESE OUT

www.reelfastfilms.com
Vancouver's challenge

www.filmchallenge.com
A national film challenge in the U.S.

www.48hourfilm.com
A national film challenge in the U.S.

www.48hourfilm challenge.com
U.K. and European film-challenge site

www.seventhsanctum.com A genre and title generator site

SUPER 8

ALTHOUGH SUPER 8 FILMMAKING HAS LOST OUT TO DV—IT JUST COULDN'T COMPETE ON PRICE OR EDITING CONVENIENCE—IT STILL HAS A DEDICATED FOLLOWING, AND NOWHERE MORE SO THAN AMONG THE ORGANIZERS AND PARTICIPANTS OF STRAIGHT8, AN INTERNATIONAL SHORT-FILM COMPETITION EXCLUSIVELY FOR SUPER 8 USERS.

▶▶ Straight8

▶▶ Planning and timing

▶▶ Adding sound

ASSIGNMENT

AIM:
✗ Produce a Super 8 movie on one roll of film without any editing, and create a soundtrack without seeing the exposed film.

CREW:
✗ Director
✗ Camera operator
✗ Storyboard artist
✗ Continuity/timer
✗ Sound designer/composer

EQUIPMENT:
✗ Super-8 camera
✗ Camera support (as required)

Started by two London-based film directors, Straight8 has a very simple premise: you register to take part and you are sent a single, numbered roll of Super 8 film. That's the easy part. Now you have to shoot your movie, on any subject you like (within the bounds of decency and the law), and return the exposed cartridge to the organizers for developing. You can include an original soundtrack on CD if you want. The first time the film is shown in public, usually at festivals such as Cannes, is the first time anyone will see it, including the makers.

So how do you shoot a three-minute film in one take with no editing, and add an original soundtrack? With planning, rehearsal—and a stopwatch.

Like any film, you have to start with an idea, which will have to be scripted and precisely storyboarded. Animators work with these types of storyboards because they have to account for every frame. Producing an image for every fraction of a second makes you appreciate economy of effort. Most Super 8 cameras have a single-frame option, so even shooting a stop-motion animation (such as claymation) is a perfectly viable option, even if it is a very slow one.

Getting your timing right is vital, because there are only 50 feet of film on a cartridge. This works out to 3 minutes 20 seconds at 18fps and 2 minutes 30 seconds at 24fps. Running out of stock before the end of the film would be very frustrating, hence the importance of the stopwatch.

Making every second count means timing each shot and rehearsing to perfection before shooting. For technical rehearsals use a video camera to try out different moves; this will give you instant feedback on the shots and a good idea of running time. When you start

COPPER COFFEE!
STORYBOARD ◀◀
Accurate storyboarding is important, as there are no second chances in this type of filmmaking.

SHOT LIST ▶▶
A shot list with precise timings is vital. It is better to shoot under the times than over. This is timed for shooting at 24fps.

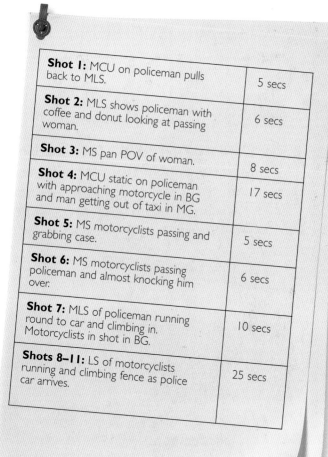

Shot 1: MCU on policeman pulls back to MLS.	5 secs
Shot 2: MLS shows policeman with coffee and donut looking at passing woman.	6 secs
Shot 3: MS pan POV of woman.	8 secs
Shot 4: MCU static on policeman with approaching motorcycle in BG and man getting out of taxi in MG.	17 secs
Shot 5: MS motorcyclists passing and grabbing case.	5 secs
Shot 6: MS motorcyclists passing policeman and almost knocking him over.	6 secs
Shot 7: MLS of policeman running round to car and climbing in. Motorcyclists in shot in BG.	10 secs
Shots 8–11: LS of motorcyclists running and climbing fence as police car arrives.	25 secs

shooting onto film, take a fresh tape and shoot the scene with the DV camera at the same time. If you can get the cameras mounted side by side, without interfering with each other, you will have an almost exact replica on video that will help with the audio.

Because Super 8 is a silent film, and the contest doesn't allow for sync sound, recording dialogue is redundant. This is something you will have to consider at the script stage. If you want dialogue as part of the film, it is best to have it all off-screen. Having a video copy of the film will also help with adding dialogue, sound effects, and composing a score. As long as the sound doesn't require very precise cues, it should work.

If taking part in Straight8 is something that appeals to you, don't rely entirely on DV; buy some Kodachrome and experiment on your own before committing to an actual shoot, and ensure that your equipment actually works.

CHECK THIS OUT

 www.straight8.net
Details of the competition plus some examples of previous entrants.

STILLS MOVIE

THE MAIN PURPOSE OF MOVIES—TELLING A STORY WITH PICTURES AND SOUND— USUALLY INVOLVES SOME SORT OF MOVEMENT, HENCE THE NAME, BUT RESTRICTING YOURSELF ONLY TO USING A MOVIE OR VIDEO CAMERA CAN LIMIT YOUR CREATIVE OPTIONS. THANKS TO DIGITAL TECHNOLOGY IT IS VERY EASY TO CREATE A MOVIE USING JUST STILLS; AFTER ALL, A MOVIE IS REALLY ONLY A SEQUENCE OF STILL IMAGES.

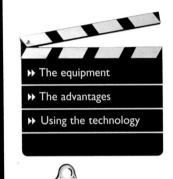

- ▸▸ The equipment
- ▸▸ The advantages
- ▸▸ Using the technology

ASSIGNMENT

AIM:
✗ Create a five- to ten-minute film using only still photographs.

CREW:
✗ Stills photographer
✗ Editor
✗ Composer

EQUIPMENT:
✗ Film or digital stills
✗ Camera
✗ Editing and/or compositing software (iMovie recommended)

Comic books, called sequential art by the late, great Will Eisner, are nothing more than a story made up of still images, yet they manage to achieve pacing through dynamic poses, composition, and the layout of panels on the pages. Photonovels use a similar concept, but with photographs, so taking the idea to the next level, using projected images, seems like a natural progression.

As with any short film, you will need to start with a script that will have to be storyboarded. The storyboard becomes the template for the movie, substituting the sketches for photographs—making it a sort of glorified animatic.

One of the advantages of making movies from stills is that equipment is no longer an issue. Of course, using a quality lens is important, but second-hand 35mm SLR cameras can be bought very cheaply (Olympus, Canon, Nikon, and Pentax all have excellent optics). Film is relatively cheap, as is having the images digitized. Alternatively, digital cameras offer excellent resolution with no film and developing outlay. Some, such as the Lumix FZ20, even have a 16:9 high-definition video resolution, so you could make an HD movie at a fraction of the usual cost. A 512Mb memory card holds more than 450 HDV stills, which should give you plenty of images to work with.

When it comes to the shoot, you are freed from a lot of the usual constraints of filmmaking—actors missing lines or marks, calculating camera moves, recording sound, feeding a large crew. Depending on the nature of the story, you can control the composition without it seeming overly static, because it already is. Taking stills while your cast acts out a scene will give the pictures more realism, but if you see something interesting, it is easy to get the actors to hold or redo a pose without having to reshoot a whole sequence.

Once you have shot all the pictures (and shoot a lot) you can start editing them together. If you use a digital camera and a Macintosh computer, you already have everything you need, in the form of Apple's iLife software (iPhoto, iMovie, GarageBand, and iDVD), to put the movie together. There are plenty of other options, including the excellent Adobe Video Collection for Windows. More economical, shareware programs for Windows users are available, but here we will concentrate on using iLife.

With all the images instantly imported into iPhoto, the best can be selected and placed into a separate album to make them easier to find. Because iPhoto and iMovie are designed to work together, the iPhoto library is visible in iMovie and the images are ready to be dropped into the timeline. Movement (panning and zooming) can be added using the Ken Burns effect (named after the documentary filmmaker). The timing of each shot is easily controlled, as are the cuts and transitions. To take the clean digital edge off the images and make it look like a film, effects such as dust and scratches can be added—but don't overdo it. A soundtrack can be made using GarageBand, and a voiceover can be added, if necessary. Once it's all edited together, it can finally be burned to a DVD, and you have your finished movie ready to show to your public.

Of course, using professional software like After Effects or Final Cut will give you more control, but it

A transformed human is indistinguishable from a real dog.

LA VIE D'UN CHIEN ◀◀

John Harden's award-winning short is made from black and white stills with a French narration (shown here with English subtitles), and has a style reminiscent of European films from the sixties (see www.johnfilms.com).

He awakens in his office, reflecting upon a night

may take you longer to learn how to use them than to create the whole film in iMovie.

No matter what software you use, try to keep the story and editing well-paced and any dialogue or voiceover believable. Have a look at *La Jetée* by Chris Martin (the film that inspired *Twelve Monkeys*) or *La Vie d'un Chien* by John Harden as examples of what can be achieved.

LA VIE D'UN CHIEN: SHOOT SCRIPT

[FADE IN on a montage of black and white still photos: Cityscapes at night. Paris. A MALE VOICE narrates. All narration will be in French; what follows here are the English subtitles.]

Night falls on Paris. Our story begins here, in a laboratory, after hours… where one man works alone.

[Deserted back streets. Through a window can be seen a man in lab coat, working at an assembly of tubing, beakers, and test tubes.]

Almost every night, the scientist works late. There is no wife expecting him at home. No close associates with whom he cares to socialize. His closest relationship is his friendship with a terrier he has liberated from his group of test subjects. He has given her the name Sylvie.

[Inside the lab. More angles of the scientist at work. His lab also holds computer terminals and a wall of steel cages, each containing a different breed of dog.]

The scientist studies the genetic structure of dogs. In the course of his work, he makes a breakthrough: a simple chemical process that will cause human chromosomes to temporarily mimic those of a dog.

[Scientist mixes formula, holds up test tube.]

The scientist tests the formula on himself. In the course of a few minutes, he is transformed.

[Scientist drinks formula, reacts – cut to shots of the other dogs watching intently through their cage bars. Scientist staggers out of the lab.]

He blunders into the night, disoriented by his new body.

[CROSS DISSOLVE a series of low-angle, blurry shots – his POV.]

Here he is buffeted by his now hyperacute senses. The sounds of the metropolis envelop him, amazing in their clarity.

[City street, with sound effects.]

Odors from the sidewalk flood his nose, a collage of vivid messages now just inches from his face.

[PAN along C/U photo of sidewalk with cigarette butts, melted Popsicle, fire hydrant…]

DUST AND SCRATCHES ◀◀

Use one of the many filters available to add dust and scratches and give your movie the look of an old film.

3D ANIMATION

MAKING SHORT MOVIES DOES NOT HAVE TO BE LIMITED TO USING CAMERAS AND ACTORS. IF YOU DON'T HAVE ACCESS TO THE PEOPLE OR EQUIPMENT REQUIRED, BUT STILL HAVE A STORY YOU WANT TO TELL, WHY NOT TRY ANIMATION? THERE ARE LOTS OF DIFFERENT STYLES AND METHODS OF CREATING ANIMATED FILMS, BUT ONE OF THE EASIEST WAYS IS WITH CURIOS LABS POSER OR DAZ|STUDIO—BOTH OF WHICH ARE ALSO EXCELLENT AS PRE-VISUALIZATION TOOLS FOR LIVE ACTION FILMS.

▸▸ New technology, expanding abilities

▸▸ Tips on using the software

Creating 3D CGI animations is usually looked upon as the preserve of highly paid geeks with very little life away from their computer monitors. This may be a fair assessment, given the complexity of the task, especially when it comes to creating human figures. But thanks to some innovative software and powerful home computers, it is possible to make excellent animated shorts with very little 3D experience.

Poser was originally designed to give digital artists a computer version of the artist's wooden mannequin. It developed to become a fully-fledged 3D character-design and artwork tool that was capable of animation. As its popularity increased, so did the content available for use in it, as well as its integration with other 3D software, such as Carrara Studio or Lightwave, and Bryce, the landscape generator. Poser will never match the CGI produced by Hollywood studios, but if you want to create a short 3D animated film with realistic humans, it is more than capable of the task. It also acts as an excellent tool for storyboards and animatics.

ASSIGNMENT

AIM:
✗ Produce three-minute character animation using Poser or DAZ|Studio.

CREW:
✗ Animator

EQUIPMENT:
✗ Macintosh or Windows computer
✗ Curious Labs Poser or Daz|Studio
✗ Daz Mimic
✗ 3D characters, clothes, and props

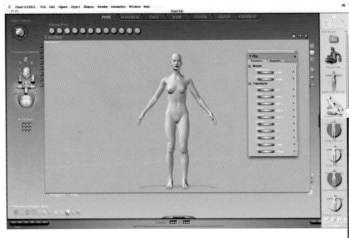

BODY ▲
Start by building your character. This example is based on DAZ's Stephanie 3.

CLOTHING ▾
Add the appropriate clothes. Use the double click to "Create New Figure" and, very importantly, each item of clothing has to be "Conformed" to the main figure so they all move together.

As most of the content developed for Poser seems to be in the fantasy and sci-fi realms, unless you are capable of creating your own 3D props, these are the genres in which it will be easiest to work. Although there is a slightly generic feel to Poser characters, they are highly customizable, so you can give them individuality, and the sheer volume of clothes and props available provides almost unlimited possibilities.

Once you have selected your model and clothes, you must make sure they are fixed to each other so that they will move together. In Poser this is known as "conforming." Once you have created them, getting the characters to move is fairly easy, although posing does take a little practice, as they have a habit of contorting themselves into very unusual positions.

Poser uses a timeline animation system with keyframes, the extreme points of an action. All animation relies on keyframes, but in cel animation the lead animator will draw these, and other artists will draw all the positions in-between. This process is known as "in-betweening" or "tweening." In Poser, as in other 3D software, the tweening is done for you. Place one pose as a keyframe in the timeline, then

ACHIEVING ANIMATION

All types of animated films are accepted in short film festivals, and 3D animation is not the only one that can easily be done at home. The following are possible with minimal equipment:

● **Cut-out and collage** A scanner and simple editing software will do the trick.

● **Stop Motion** Claymation (for example, Wallace and Grommet) can be done with a simple digital still camera and basic software. Super 8 and DV are also popular for doing this.

● **Flash** Originally designed for making Web banners, this software has become an extremely powerful, relatively easy to use animation tool. Drawing skills are useful. Try Toon Boom Studio for proper animation tools using this file format.

Check out *The Complete Animation Course* by Chris Patmore (Barron's Educational Series, Inc., 2003) for a good introduction to all forms of animation.

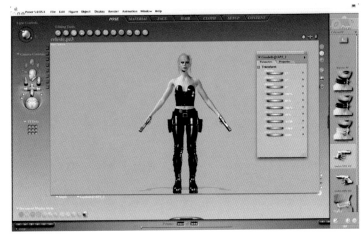

ACCESSORIZE ▲
Add hair, makeup, and props to bring the character to life.

CHECK THESE OUT

www.curiouslabs. com Home of Poser software

www.daz3d.com Home of Poser characters, clothes, and props, DAZ|Studio, DAZ|Mimic, and Bryce

www.eovia.com Carrara Studio, 3D software that integrates with Poser

www.poserpros.com For models, clothes, and props

www.renderosity. com For models, clothes, and props

www.rdna.com For models, clothes, and props

PROJECTS

SETTING THE SCENE ▲
Place the character in a scene. This one is from DAZ. You can create your own with 3D programs such as Bryce, Carrara Studio, Vue d'Espirit, or Lightwave, which all work with Poser.

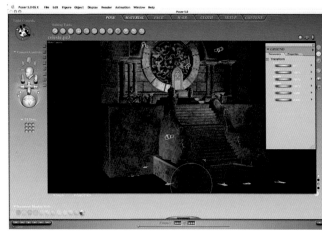

LIGHTING ▲
Give the scene some suitable lighting. There are many pre-set lighting arrangements available from the sites listed.

place another pose at an appropriate place, and the movement will be completed. A huge number of pre-set poses are available to buy over the Internet, which makes the job even easier. Cameras can also be animated, so creating those (overdone) bullet-time effects is very easy.

If you want to create talking heads, Poser comes with a collection of basic phonemes (mouth shapes), but to make it easier and more realistic use DAZ|Mimic. This takes a sound file and creates the poses that can then be applied to any Poser character.

You can also easily create a green-screen background for your animation and incorporate it into a live-action movie. Poser character animations can also be integrated into other software such as landscape generators like Bryce.

Rendering any animation is a slow process and Poser is no exception. Serious Poser animators use other 3D software such as Carrara Studio or Lightwave for rendering as they produce better images, but Poser's rendering engine will produce results that are more than adequate for initial attempts.

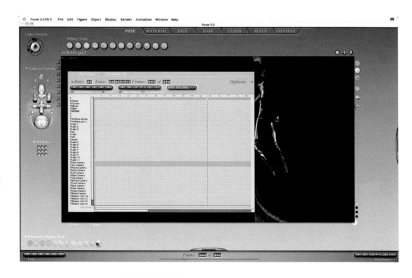

FINE TUNING ▲
Fine tune your sequence using the Animation Palette (available under the Windows menu).

ACTION ▲

The hardest part is posing the characters. Luckily, a good number of poses are available as starting points. Poser animation uses key frames so you only need to set the extremes of each action. Calculate the time it takes for the action to happen and click the + in the bottom right-hand corner.

CHANGING VIEWPOINT ▲

Once the movement sequence is completed, you can "shoot" it from different angles using another camera, which can also be animated using key frames.

RENDERING ▼

Once your animation is completed, you have to render it. The render engine in Poser does a fair job, although it may need some experimentation. Save it in a format that will work with your editing software—DV is the most common.

DIALOGUE ▲ ▶▶

If you want to add lip-synched dialogue, it is made easy using DAZ Mimic. This takes a recording (in WAV or AIFF format) and creates all the appropriate mouth shapes. This program will save you days of work.

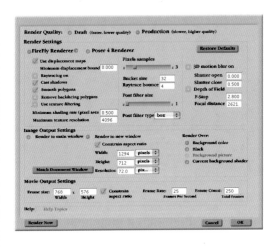

GETTING IT SEEN

One of the biggest parts of a Hollywood movie budget is dedicated to marketing and distribution. Having spent millions on getting the film made, the studios need people to see it to recoup their costs.

The whole marketing machine is a complex one, made up of focus groups, advertising specialists, and media experts. They use every method at their disposal to entice the public to part with their money at the local movie theater, no matter how good or bad the film is.

Low-budget filmmakers can't match the resources (financial or otherwise) of the big studios, but they do have assets that the studios often lack—imagination, originality, and the freedom that comes from having nothing to lose.

Of course, you want people to see your film—that is, after all, why you made it— but your target audience isn't going to be the Saturday-night popcorn crowd. If your ambition is to be a filmmaker, you need people with lots of money to see your movie, to see your capabilities, and to give you the financial backing to work on bigger projects.

This section covers some of the ways you can get your films out to the toughest audience, the jaded industry people who have seen it all, and usually know it all. But as William Goldman keeps asserting, in Hollywood "Nobody knows anything." And that goes pretty much for the entire international film industry.

Just being a good cook isn't enough; presentation is a big part of a chef's success. And so it is with filmmaking. Although talent will usually shine through, it is the presentation of your work that will get it noticed. The following pages will give you some ideas using readily accessible methods, including festivals and the Internet, that won't cause you to go deeply into debt.

MARKETING

One of the big problems with short films is the lack of a lucrative market. Short films used to be shown in movie theaters before the main features, but nowadays the only ones that are seen are advertisements and trailers.

The following pages suggest some places to get your movie seen, but before that you will need to create an attractive package, giving it a chance by providing an edge over the competition.

▸▸ The press kit

▸▸ Presentation is key

PRESS GANG Your most important marketing tool is the press kit. This has to be multipurpose, serving the media, potential buyers/distributors, and festival organizers. No matter what design or packaging you choose, it has to contain: a copy of the film; a trailer for the film; a written synopsis of the film; bios of the key cast and crew members; and photos. You should also include some posters or flyers. If the package is going to the media (radio, TV, newspapers), include a sheet of ten frequently asked questions, with the answers.

PACKAGE BREAKDOWN The design of your package creates the all-important first impression. You are never going to be able to compete with the majors, but try to be creative; go beyond using a standard folder of loose pages with a DVD or videotape tacked on. Make the overall design consistent with any graphics used in the movie. Try to keep all the written info bound together, so individual sheets don't get lost. Make sure the package is robust enough to withstand handling. There is no point creating something that is stunning but disintegrates as soon as it is touched. With the low price and high quality of digital printing, you should be able to do something impressive without breaking the bank.

Include the finished film. Technology changes quickly, but DVD is your best option. Most people seem to have players and a lot of computers can also play DVDs. If you are concentrating just on the local market, you don't have to worry about format (PAL/NTSC). If you are going for international distribution, you will have to create both versions and make sure there is no region encoding. Include a trailer for the film on the DVD and make sure the disc is easy to navigate. Your DVD will have lots of free space so you can also include a digital version of the press kit. Use formats such as PDF or RTF, because not everyone uses Microsoft Office. More importantly, make sure both Mac and Windows computers can read the disc. Besides a DVD, you may want to include a CD that contains all the digital files (photos, synopsis, etc.), and a version of the film as a QuickTime movie that can be seen on non-DVD equipped computers. You have to cover every eventuality.

Written material needs to include a synopsis of the film, although three would be better—long, medium, and short. The short one can be as few as 50–75 words, while the long one can be as much as a page. The actual length will be partly dictated by your film. Write simply and concisely, avoiding too many superlatives. You are writing an outline of the

FAQs ◀◀

Frequently asked questions are a list of obvious questions journalists might ask. Make the questions relevant and the answers simple. It is also a chance to give your best interview, as you have plenty of time to come up with witty answers.

FAQs

1. Where did you get the idea? Is it autobiographical?
As with many stories, an element of personal experience is involved. I did have a moment of "Is this what my life has amounted to…" in a similar parking lot, and elaborated it into a short story that was later adapted into a screenplay.

2. How long did it take to shoot?
It was actually shot over one weekend, but a couple of years passed between when it was originally written and when it was made. In fact, I was intending to use my own children in the film but they grew too big. There was a lot of pre-production, so we knew exactly what we were going to do. Shooting on digital was a huge time saver, too.

3. How did you cast the lead actors?
They are friends who happen to be married to each other. They have done a lot of television work. In fact, one of the reasons we had to shoot as quickly as possible was because they are busy with paying acting jobs.

4. What about the children?
My own kids were too big so I asked among my friends. Despite the film maxim about working with children, I find them easy to direct as they are very natural. If you make it a game for them, everyone enjoys it.

5. What was the budget?
There was no budget as such. It actually cost less than $100, including feeding everyone. Of course, if everyone had been paid for their time that would give a completely different figure.

6. Is this your first movie?
It's the first movie I've made that I felt worthy of showing in public. I have shot several other shorts within limited time periods, but without any proper pre-production. It taught me how to work fast, and that it is better to have a plan.

7. What is your next project?
I have several projects in various stages of development at the moment.

story, not a review. If you don't feel confident, find a copywriter to do it for you. They should also be able to use correct grammar and spelling, both of which are important if you want to appear professional. Cast and crew bios may require even more creativity if you are relatively unknown or inexperienced. Don't lie or over-exaggerate, but find ways to make the most of what you have. "First-time filmmaker" and "untrained actors" work if the film is good.

The FAQs with answers will make it easier for journalists to write a piece without having to leave their desks. It also ensures that they have the right information.

You will need photos of the principal cast and crew, and a selection of production shots. These can include behind-the-scenes shots and photos of the actors taken during rehearsals. A good digital camera should do the job. You can take prints from it, and magazines will need the images digitized for laying out anyway. These can go on the CD or DVD.

Always go for quality over quantity in all the material in your presentation. You are dealing with busy people who won't take the time to sift through a mountain of pages and pictures to find something worth using. In the end it is the film that counts, no matter how slick your presentation.

SYNOPSIS ▶▶
The length of the synopsis will be dictated by the length of the movie. Make the short one intriguing, with the longer ones revealing more of the story, but never giving everything away. After all, you want them to watch it!

Short synopsis
Crisis? What Crisis?
Matt is entering middle age. His arrival in the parking lot of a well-known furniture superstore sparks an existential crisis that will deeply affect him.

PUBLICITY

Publicity has to start before you begin filming. Local newspapers need to fill their pages with articles other than domestic disputes. Let them know you are shooting a film, especially if there is a human-interest angle to it. "Local people aiming for Cannes." You can even supply them with the photos and copy. If they publish it, you will have a clipping for the press kit.

Long synopsis
Crisis? What Crisis?
Matt's fortieth birthday is approaching fast. He has a loving wife, two beautiful children, and a comfortable domestic existence. Life doesn't place too many demands on him, but there are some he'd rather avoid and today he must fulfill a promise he made to his wife and accept the inevitable. After surviving a journey from hell, he arrives at his destination (the parking lot of a well-known furniture superstore), where he has to face his demons, only to suffer an existential crisis that will deeply affect him and those who love him.

Medium synopsis
Crisis? What Crisis?
Matt's fortieth birthday is approaching fast. He has a loving wife, two beautiful children, and a comfortable domestic existence. Life doesn't place too many demands on him, but there are some he'd rather avoid and today he is faced with one he can no longer put off. In the parking lot of a well-known furniture superstore he suffers an existential crisis that will deeply affect him and those he loves.

CALLING CARD

Some people spend their whole career making short films because they enjoy the format and find it the best medium in which to express their ideas. Most filmmakers, however, use them as a training ground and a calling card before working on larger projects.

The *modus operandi* is much like that for marketing, described on the previous pages, but the focus is slightly different. Instead of the

- ▸▸ Using your film to attract backing
- ▸▸ Make a showreel
- ▸▸ Networking

movie and its story being the most important element of the package, it has to concentrate on you and your talent. This does not lessen the value of the movie in any way, because ultimately that is what you will be judged on, but you are selling yourself and not the film. You are also targeting different people. Instead of trying to impress distributors or festival organizers, you want the movie to be seen by producers or financiers.

In reality, your first short film is not likely to be good enough to convince a major producer or studio to give you enough to make a feature. It is more likely to show your potential to backers for another short. These could be equipment-rental companies, labs, effects houses—the places that can help you to create a more professional-looking film. You can go to them and say, "Look, this is what I did on a miniDV with no crew. Imagine what I could do with your cameras/film/processing." Facilities houses are always on the lookout for hot new talent to which they can attach their names; they figure that if they look after you, if or when you make it big you will remember

their help and give them more substantial business.

This sort of sponsorship is not the only way to get another movie made. There are all sorts of arts grants available, and having some previous work to show will definitely help your case. However, grants do come with all sorts of conditions attached, so they may not be something you want to pursue.

If you really want to go for the big producers, you will need more than one short film, unless it is the greatest thing since *Citizen Kane*. You need a showreel. This is like a trailer for all your work, showing cleverly edited excerpts of the best bits of directing, camerawork, or sound design. With DVD-authoring software, a showreel can include not only the standard edited highlights version, but also the full-length versions of your movies. That way, if the viewer's interest is aroused, he or she can choose whether or not to watch more.

Even the best showreel in the world is not going to help if you can't get the right people to see it. Ingenuity and persistence are two

INTERNATIONAL ARTS GRANTS

Australian Film Commission:
www.afc.gov.au/funding/

British Council:
www.britishcouncil.org/arts-film-funding.htm

Canada Council for the Arts:
www.canadacouncil.ca/mediaarts/

Cinema for Tolerance:
www.cinemafortolerance.org/grants.htm

Film Arts Foundation:
www.filmarts.org/grants

Global Film Initiative: **www.globalfilm.org** (feature films only)

Manitoba Arts Council:
www.artscouncil.mb.ca/english/vis_grantind.html

Moxie Films:
www.moxie-films.com

National Endowment for the Arts:
www.nea.gov

Princess Grace Awards:
www.pgfusa.com/awards/film/

Roy W. Dean Film and Writing Grants:
www.fromtheheartproductions.com

UK Film Council:
www.ukfilmcouncil.org.uk/funding/

Check your local or state arts council as they usually have film and video funding.

prerequisites, as is a thick skin to counter constant rejection. So how do you get your work to producers? Cold calling and unsolicited mailings do not work—you have more chance of winning a lottery. Because the movie community is relatively small, networking is an excellent way to start meeting people. Joining an independent filmmaking organization or society, such as Raindance, gives you a chance to meet like-minded people. Once you start to become familiar with other filmmakers, there is a chance that you will be introduced to someone who is genuinely interested in what you are doing. "Who you know and not what you know" will get you a long way. Just remember to stay enthusiastic and passionate, and carry a DVD or two with you at all times.

Whatever method you want to use to get your film in front of a producer, from networking to stealth, you have to make sure you have something worth showing, which is where competitions and festivals come in handy.

FESTIVALS

Festivals and competitions probably provide the best opportunities to have your film seen and gain some sort of recognition for all your hard work. These range from high-profile events like Sundance to small local ones. Naturally, you'd like to be seen at Sundance or Cannes, but then so does everyone. Picking a smaller, local festival or competition is a better place to start.

Given the sheer number of festivals and competitions, it is a good idea to do some market research before you start. Entering your movie into a festival or competition and having it rejected without explanation can feel like a personal slight, but it may have been simply because you didn't read the entry requirements. With hundreds or even thousands of movies being entered into events, you are not likely to receive an explanation or personal reply, if you get any reply at all. If you receive any

feedback beyond acknowledgement of receipt, you are doing well.

To begin you will need a list of festivals. A good place to start is www.filmfestivals.com as it lets you search for festivals by area and/or date, then gives you all the information you need or links to where you can get it. Look at the entry requirements and at the type of films that have been entered or shown on previous occasions. Although festivals may call themselves "open," they usually have a preference for particular types of films, while others are genre festivals. If your movie is sci-fi it makes sense to look for sci-fi festivals, but if its themes are broader and less obviously sci-fi you may be able to cross it over into other genres.

The other thing to look for is format. More and more festivals are accepting movies on DV, and with the arrival of affordable HDDV cameras and digital projectors, this trend is likely to increase. You are not very likely to find an outlet for Super 8 films, except

FESTIVAL SCREENINGS ▶▶
Film festivals come in all shapes and sizes, from the small and intimate to the major media circuses. Small festivals are a lot more flexible about formats, and give plenty of opportunities to exchange ideas with other filmmakers.

for Super 8-specific competitions, mainly because of projection problems.

Many festivals ask for an entry fee for your film. At this stage you need to make a decision about whether you want to part with your cash and take a chance. The bigger the festival, the higher the fee, with no guarantee that your movie will even be looked at when it is submitted. You also need to see what the fee entitles you to. At the very minimum you should get tickets to the showing. Also be aware that there are some unscrupulous people out there running festivals that don't ever happen, or promise more than the fee merits—research is vital.

COMPETITIONS Most festivals will run some sort of competition in conjunction with the main event, although not all competitions are linked to festivals. Competitions are often theme- or genre-based, like the festivals, so it is important to find one that is suitable. If you are a procrastinator, like most novice filmmakers, competitions are great motivators. Deadlines are a great way to get those creative juices flowing, and help make you more decisive.

As with festivals, before you fork out any money for a competition (some do charge) look at what they are offering for the fee. See if there is any history behind the competition, or its organizers. Filmmaking is a small community and a bad reputation soon becomes general knowledge. Always read the terms and conditions before submitting your film, to make sure you aren't signing away all the rights to your work.

If possible, have a look at previous winners. This will give you an idea not only of what the judges are looking for, but also of the level of competition, which may help you decide whether it is worth entering or not. The important thing is to get the film made in the first place.

If you can't find a reasonably local competition, where you can actually talk to organizers and see the finished movies, there are plenty of competitions online. Some of them, such as www.triggerstreet.com and www.moviesaskew.com (run by Kevin Spacey and Kevin Smith, respectively), are very popular. For more on movies on the Internet, turn the page.

MINI CINE ▲
Taking the home cinema out of the home and into a festival, the organizers of the Sci-Fi-London Film Festival created a mini-cine where short films were shown continuously for free, with audiences voting for their favorite. Initiatives like this help keep short films alive and in the public eye.

FESTIVAL ENTRY REQUIREMENTS ▶▶

Every film festival has slightly different entry requirements, so read the submission information carefully. At the right is an edited example of the requirements of the Raindance Film Festival.

All festival submission forms require a similar amount of information. Legal requirements may differ from country to country, so it is best to ensure that you have everything concerning rights in order.

1. The format the movie was shot on. This can be taken into consideration when it comes to final selection, for projection reasons.

2. These are the highest quality standard formats available in most cinemas, although an increasing number have digital projectors that will show DVDs.

3. Some festivals specialize in specific genres (e.g., horror, sci-fi) but some categories are more open.

4. Take this from your already prepared Press Kit.

5. Listing your name can look either impressive or smack of amateurism. It worked for Robert Rodriguez.

6. For your first efforts you will probably not be able to complete this, but if your film is shown at the festival, there is a chance someone will approach you.

7. Some festivals demand exclusives, while others want quality. Don't lie, as filmmaking is a very small world.

8. This is not a Faustian deal, so you are not signing your life away, but make sure you read all the terms and conditions carefully, and get advice if you have any doubts.

CHECK THESE OUT

Festivals

Raindance
www.raindance.co.uk

Sci Fi London www.sci-fi-london.com

TromaDance
www.tromadance.com

www.withoutabox.com
Online service for entering festivals

Festival entry requirements

Submission form
[requires the following information]:
- Film details
1 ● Originating format
2 ● Festival screening format
- Optical sound format
- Aspect ratio
3 ● Genre
4 ● Short synopsis
- Submitting party contact information
- Print source
5 ● Credits
6 ● Available rights
7 ● Screening history
8 ● Submission fees and agreement with the terms of the Raindance Festival

Submission deadline
- Films will be accepted from 9 March [of the year of the Festival] and no later than 1 July of that year

Submission format
- Films must be submitted on DVD or VHS only: Raindance has the capability to screen 35mm with optical soundtracks, Beta Sp, DigiBeta, DVD, 1/2 in. VHS. All tape formats must be PAL. Their facilities do not support 16mm, Super 16, or double head formats
- The title, screening format, and running time must be clearly labeled on the cover
- Submitted copies will not be returned but may be collected from Raindance after the festival

Submission eligibility ●
- All submissions must have been completed after 1 September [of the previous year]
- Films must not have been released in the UK on any format
- Submission packages must include a preview copy, a completed Raindance Festival Submission Form, the correct submission fee, and a Press Kit containing a 200 word synopsis, full cast and crew credits, a director's biography, and a CD with a director's photograph and two production stills
- All films in a language other than English must be subtitled in English
- Exploitation and pornography genres are not eligible

Selection of films ●
Submissions are reviewed and selected under the following criteria:

- Quality of narrative and production values
- Independent nature of the production
- Limitations and availability of screening slots
- Availability of film rights for distribution

Raindance endeavors to complete all selection procedures by 1 September [of that year] and inform all Submitting Parties, in writing, if their film has been successful or not at that time. Successful submissions will receive correspondence that will include important information on shipping the print or tape to the festival, press and publicity, guest accreditation, contact information, and how to make the most of participating in the festival. A selected print or tape must be received at Raindance no later than five days prior to its scheduled screening date.

Each festival has its own rules about what it will accept and how the submissions should be made. The Raindance Festival shows a broad spectrum of genres that must adhere to the independent filmmaking ethos.

Some festivals have a reputation for not looking at submissions and just pocketing the fee. Raindance's selection criteria is simple and they have a team of viewers that watch everything sent to them before making a list of those that will be shown.

INTERNET

If the vicarious thrills of the competition circuit aren't for you, one of the easiest ways to get your film seen is to put it on the Internet. You can send your movie to one of the many existing Web sites, such as atomfilms.com or triggerstreet.com, or you can go completely independent and run your own site.

- ▶▶ Established sites
- ▶▶ Setting up your own site
- ▶▶ Generating traffic

Well-established sites, such as triggerstreet.com, have a huge audience, mostly of other filmmakers, improving the chances of your movie being seen by the right people. This is especially true for triggerstreet, as all newly posted films get a chance to be reviewed by other filmmakers as part of the conditions of posting to the site. Getting feedback from your peers is a useful way to find out if what you have done is any good, with the added bonus that you won't be humiliated in person.

Of course, if you are shying away from the competition and festival circuit, these sites may not be of much interest to you. Unfortunately, timidity is not a good quality in a filmmaker. The whole point of making a movie is for it to be seen, and anyone who tells you otherwise is either trying to fool you or is fooling himself.

GOING INDY Remaining independent, with your own Web site, has its own range of pros and cons beyond independence. Before diving in and making your own site, you should consider some of the following points, most of which may seem obvious or commonsense.

Do you have a domain name? Most of the good .com names have already been registered. Look at some of the other possibilities; .tv is a good one for movies. Don't make the name too long or too hard to remember: it's going to be tricky enough getting traffic to your site without making it difficult to type the name correctly.

This brings up the problem of getting people to your site. With billions of Web sites on the net, getting people to see your film needs ingenuity and a certain amount of luck. Meta tags are your first line of attack: with the

MOVIES ASKEW ▲
Film director Kevin Smith (*Clerks*, *Dogma*) is doing his part to keep independent filmmaking alive by running a Web-based short film competition. Definitely leftfield.

ATOM FILMS ▲
One of the original short film Web sites, catering to all tastes and genres. Probably some of the highest quality shorts on the Net.

right words placed there, search engines will find you, but your position in the search list will rely on the number of hits the site has had, so you end up in a kind of Catch-22 situation. The best way to generate traffic is to get a buzz going and let word of mouth (or e-mail) do it for you. It does help if you have something worth showing, but hype worked for *The Blair Witch Project*. E-mailing everyone you know and getting them to tell everyone they know will soon spread the word, and while this method is sometimes frowned on, if the message is just sent to people with whom you are acquainted, it shouldn't cause too much harm. Don't inadvertently attach a virus.

Three important aspects of a Web site, often overlooked, are content, navigation, and speed. This book isn't about how to create Web sites, but ensure that the content is easy to find, easy to access, and worth watching in the first place. Although broadband is very common, there are still people using dial-up accounts, so you should cater to lower-spec users. This means making sure pages load quickly. Don't make them too graphics intensive, which is advisable from the design aspect anyway. Macromedia Flash makes very interesting interactive sites, but they can be slow to display. Always make two versions of your film available— one for dial-up users and one for broadband—

and make sure they are in a format that everyone can view; QuickTime is best for this as it does not need any special server software and the viewer is free to download. It is also possible to convert your films into the ubiquitous Flash format using a program like Flix from Wildform.

One other aspect to consider when creating your Web site is its purpose. Is it going to serve as an online showcase, or are you going to use it as a commercial venture? Initially it is probably best to keep it as a showcase until the quality of your work, or your reputation, makes revenue a possibility. This can range from pay-for-view to selling DVDs, but take one step at a time, and start by getting a finished film online.

CHECK THESE OUT

www.apple.com/quicktime QuickTime is the underlying technology for digital video on computers and the Internet

www.macromedia.com Web-creation software

www.microsoft.com/windows media Player and server media software

www.real.com Real provides media streaming

www.wildform.com Convert standard video to the Flash format

www.amazefilms.com Internet film distribution

www.atomfilms.com Atom Films online movies

http://filmwatcher.com Short film portal

www.moviesaskew.com Kevin Smith's online film community

www.triggerstreet.com Kevin Spacey's online film community

GET YOUR FILM SEEN ON THE INTERNET

1 Write a brilliant script and make the movie, bearing in mind that shorter is better.

2 Find a site that caters to your genre of film.

3 Follow all the submission guidelines. Pay particular attention to the rules regarding rights and clearance.

4 Get all your friends, and their friends, to watch and vote for it.

5 Set up your own Web site to host your films.

6 Save the file in a suitable streaming format (QuickTime, Real, Windows Media). Don't make the files too big, or offer two different-sized versions. Remember that QuickTime is free.

RIGHTS

In simple terms, you own the copyright to any original work that you create, unless and until you sign those rights over to another person or organization. It's then that the whole issue of rights becomes murky and filled with lots of legalities and jargon that seem mainly to benefit the lawyers.

You may not need to prove or defend the originality of your work while it remains in the

▸▸ Register your script

▸▸ Staying within the law

▸▸ Product placement

non-profit realm of private showings, but the sooner you learn to protect yourself, the better. This starts at the script-writing stage and usually involves registering your script with an organization such as the Writers' Guild of America (WGA; www.wga.org) or a similar local organization. There is usually a fee for this, and it can be done on the Internet. The chance that a story similar to your own brilliantly original idea already exists is high, but having your screenplay registered is still your best protection.

Of course, if your screenplay is for your own episode of *Star Wars*, you may have trouble registering it. That doesn't stop you from making it as a fan film, you just can't sell it or make money from it—unless of course George Lucas gives his permission and blessing.

Material protected under copyright can go beyond identifiable characters to include any recognizable product, work of art, or piece of

music. Different countries have different rules, but it is best to abide by international copyright law, just to be on the safe side. We live in extremely litigious times, and a slight oversight in getting proper clearances could stymie the release of your breakout film for years, with the lawyers being the only ones making money. If you are going to have well-known products in your shots, get permission from the copyright owners or the manufacturers before you start shooting.

If you are clever, you should be able to turn it to your advantage, particularly if there is another major competitive brand. If your star needs to drink a can of cola, you can approach your preferred brand and ask them not only to supply the permission but also all the cans necessary for the shoot. Product placement is big business, so why not get a slice of that action and cover yourself at the same time?

The use of music has been covered on pages 98–99, but be aware that any songs playing on a radio or stereo in the scene are still classified as a performance, so will need (expensive) clearance. By now you will know not to have such electronic devices on during filming anyway, simply as a continuity issue; they are added in post-production.

For your first attempts at making films, it is probably best not to worry too much about eliminating all branding from the shoot, as it is unlikely to be seen by the general public. However, if your talent and/or ambition are so great that you are confident of the work being shown in public, then it is best to do the right thing from the start. You might be able to claim "fair usage," especially on not-for-profit (as opposed to not profitable) movies, in the sense that the items are in common use in everyday life, and provided they are not an integral part of the story, you will probably be safe, although restricted in where you can show the finished film.

Read the small print

"I hereby irrevocably and unconditionally waive any so-called "moral rights of authors" in the Programmes and such rights under section 77 and section 80 of the Copyright Designs and Patents Act 1988 as I now have or hereafter acquire in relation to the Programmes."

This simply means you are signing your work away, so you'd better hope they are paying you well.

The whole subject of copyright is huge and complex and fills many large and very dull books. If you have doubts, seek legal advice; it may save you a lot of money and aggravation in the long run. That goes for any contracts or agreements you are asked to sign as well. Distributors are out to make money above anything else, and even if you assign all the rights to them, you can be pretty sure that if litigation results from your oversight, they will send the lawyers to you. Bear that in mind before you sign away the rights to your work.

Always err on the side of caution, and remember that even if it is a lo-no budget film, the law does not look on poverty as a defense.

CHECK THESE OUT

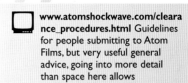

www.atomshockwave.com/clearance_procedures.html Guidelines for people submitting to Atom Films, but very useful general advice, going into more detail than space here allows

www.marklitwak.com Entertainment lawyer

www.npa.org.uk New Producers Alliance: Membership provides legal advice on movie-related issues such as contracts and copyright

www.raindance.co.uk Home of the Raindance Festival and courses and services for filmmakers, including script registration

www.wga.org Writers Guild of America for registering screenplays

Clearance and Copyright Michael C. Donaldson (Silman-James Press (2nd ed.), 2003)

Getting Permission: How to License and Clear Copyrighted Materials Online and Off Richard Stim (Nolo Press, 2000)

Rights Clearances for Film and Television Productions Stephen Edwards (available from www.pact.co.uk)

Typical contract (for festival entrance)

By submitting an Entry, you hereby (a) represent that you are the sole author and owner of your Entry and your Entry is under no restriction, contractual or otherwise, which will prevent The Festival's use of it or you from meeting your obligations; (b) agree that the Entry shall be free of all liens, encumbrances, and claims of third parties; (c) acknowledge and agree that nothing in your Entry infringes on any copyrights or trademarks, or violates any person's rights of privacy or publicity and that you have obtained all necessary releases and permissions; and (d) agree to comply with these official rules and the terms of service.

Entries determined by The Festival to infringe on any intellectual property rights, or other rights, will be disqualified and no refunds will be given. All materials submitted become property of The Festival (but not the intellectual property rights, as described below).

RIGHTS: As part of the entry process, you must execute the official Submission Agreement. Please review this Submission Agreement carefully! By executing the Submission Agreement, you will be, among other things, promising that you have obtained all necessary rights and clearances in connection with your film.

If your film is chosen as a finalist, The Festival will have the non-exclusive right to exploit your film in any way, in its sole discretion (but not the obligation to exploit your film in any way). In addition, derivative rights to your film will be licensed to The Festival for a minimum period of two years, as set forth in the Submission Agreement.

If you do not obtain all rights and fully complete the Submission Agreement, your film will not be considered for entry.

This refers to the physical medium the film was sent on, not the movie itself.

"Non-exclusive" is a very important term as it allows you to show it at other places.

Two years is a fairly standard length of time for a festival to use your work, although it doesn't state a maximum period. Remember, if you are at this stage, your work is being promoted at no expense to yourself—so it is a small price to pay.

MOVING TO FEATURES

Once you've shot one, two, or more short films and are starting to receive the recognition you knew you deserved, you may want to move on to a more ambitious project—a feature film. Although the principles are the same, at least technically, working with the enlarged canvas of a feature requires a different approach.

▸▸ Ready to move on?

▸▸ Upgrading equipment

▸▸ More time, more money

STORY A short film, like a short story, is a vignette from a much larger, ongoing series of events, although complete within itself. A feature requires more exposition. Characters need to be fully developed, relationships and settings established. Telling a story in 90-plus minutes gives you the time to do this, but in that space you also have to get your idea across and keep the audience enthralled, entertained, scared, or whatever your intention is. For many filmmakers this is a natural format, one with which they feel most comfortable, while others revel in the short format. If you find short films too restricting, full length could be for you. Just make sure that you have a strong script before you start any other aspect of the production.

SHOOTING If you are going to all the trouble of making a feature-length film, you want to be sure it is seen by as wide an audience as possible. You are making them sit and watch for an hour and a half so you need to ensure that image quality is good, and this entails using the best cameras you can get. You don't have to use film—some high-profile features have been shot on the Canon XL1—but the cameras do have to be of at least that standard. With the new HDDV cameras coming out, that should not be a problem. Beyond them is the new range of professional HD cameras. Manufacturers of these cameras are very eager for them to be used to gain market acceptance, so if they like your script it may be possible to negotiate special deals.

One of the big differences between shooting a feature and a short is the time it takes, and therefore the cost and commitment involved. However long your ten-minute movie took, a feature will take at least nine times as long, but realistically more—depending on the nature of the screenplay. A lot will depend on the logistics involved in getting all the cast and crew in the same place at the same time, and that place (the location) being available on the same day as the people. This is where the time is eaten up—in pre-production—which is why it is very important to start putting into practice all the right working methods from your very first short. If you can't organize a small shoot, you don't stand a chance on something bigger.

Your rehearsal time will be expanded, as there will be more scenes and more lines to learn. The time for shooting each setup should be about the same as for the short film, unless you are going for more involved lighting or complex set pieces. You may want to shoot more coverage, especially if you are using video, which will extend your schedule. The longest job is going to be post-production, with hours more footage to cut and a longer story to pull together. Every aspect is just going to take longer.

If you are without any funding, your job is going to be that much harder. Getting someone to give up a weekend or two is not difficult, but persuading them to commit to a feature is another matter. A lot of lo-no budget films struggle and fail because of this. If you are relying on people to work for nothing, be as flexible as you can with your shooting schedule and your projected completion date, and do as much of it as you can yourself.

Ideally, your short films should have snared you some funding or sponsorship. If you have money, don't fall into the trap of spending it all on equipment and sets, neglecting the cast and crew. They are the ones making your movie, not the camera. Remember this and they will be loyal and give you more than you expect.

Whatever you decide to do—short, feature, drama, documentary—go do it. If you don't know where to start, try stimulating your imagination with some of the projects on the preceding pages.

CHECK THESE OUT

The Guerrilla Film Makers' Movie Blueprint Chris Jones (Continuum International Publishing Group, 2003)

Raindance Producers' Lab Lo-To-No Budget Filmmaking Elliot Grove (Focal Press, 2004)

Make Your Own Damn Movie Lloyd Kaufman (L.A. Weekly Books, 2003)

Rebel Without a Crew Robert Rodriguez (Plume Books, 1996)

Making Movies Sidney Lumet (Vintage (reprint ed.), 1996)

10 GOLDEN RULES FOR GETTING YOUR FILM SEEN

1 The first rule for getting your film seen is to have a great screenplay.

2 The second rule is to have a really great screenplay.

3 The third rule is to use the best equipment you can.

4 The fourth rule is to use the best talent you can.

5 The fifth rule is to have perfect sound on the film.

6 The sixth rule is to have the film in a format that can be shown in a movie theater.

7 The seventh rule is to follow all the submission guidelines for the festivals you enter.

8 The eighth rule is to network and meet as many industry people as possible.

9 The ninth rule is to be passionate and enthusiastic, but thick-skinned.

10 The tenth rule is to make sure your screenplay is THE BEST.

GLOSSARY

ADR (automatic dialogue replacement) Re-recording dialogue in a studio to match what is on screen. Used to improve sound quality.

Alpha mask/channel Provides transparency around an object on a digital image.

Ambient sound Background noise recorded to add atmosphere to a soundtrack. Also known as "atmos" and "wildtrack."

Animatics Storyboard filmed with sound to give sense of a movie's pacing. Can also be simple 3D animation to demonstrate complicated action sequences.

Animation Films made from a sequence of individual images that are either drawn, modeled, or created on a computer.

Audition Test piece by an actor to get a role in a film or play.

Auteur A somewhat pretentious name given to certain filmmakers/directors.

CCD (charge couple device) Simply put, this is what converts light into image in a DV camera—but it's much more complicated than that. The best cameras have 3 CCDs. The latest cameras come with 16:9 chips for filming native widescreen.

Cel (cellulose acetate) A sheet of transparent material used in traditional animation.

Celluloid The base material of movie film.

Chroma key Replacing a large area of flat color (usually blue or green) with another image. Also known as blue screen or green screen.

Cinematography Cinema photography—the art of using lights and cameras for motion pictures.

CGI (computer-generated imagery) Any images created by a computer, usually 3D for special effects or animation.

Color grading Balancing color to improve continuity between different shooting times or lighting. Also used for adding color effects to film or video. Also called color correction or color timing.

Continuity Ensuring that everything on screen looks the same from take to take.

Copyright An artist's legal right to control the use and reproduction of his or her work. In some countries it is seen as the right to copy.

Crane Grip equipment with a long jib that allows the camera to be moved to a greater height.

Credits List of who did what on a movie.

DAT (digital audio tape) Digital recording system that uses small cassettes.

DAZ|Studio A 3D software for creating character animation. Poser is a similar program.

Dialogue The spoken words in a movie.

DigiBeta Short for Digital Betacam, a proprietry high resolution video format from Sony.

Digital zoom Enlarges an image to make it appear as though a long lens was used. Causes degradation of the picture.

Distribution Getting your movie shown in as many cinemas or broadcasts as possible.

Documentary A factual film on any topic that is not a work of fiction.

Dolly A camera support with wheels, or running on a track, to give smooth movement.

Dubbing Adding extra sounds on top of other sounds. Replacing one language dialogue with another language. Copying from one tape to another.

DV (digital video) Any system that records moving images as digital information (ones and zeroes). Does not lose quality when copied. Popular formats are miniDV, HDV, DVCAM, DVCPro, Digital Betacam.

Editing Putting all the various shots and elements of the movie together into a coherent whole.

EP (extended play) The name given to vinyl records that are too long to qualify as singles.

Feature film A movie that is usually anywhere between 75 and 200+ minutes in length.

Film A motion picture, or the celluloid material used to make the motion picture.

Filter Either a piece of glass or gelatine that goes over the lens and changes the color and/or the amount of light reaching the film or tape. Software filters serve a similar function but after shooting. They can also apply special effects.

Focus Adjusting the elements in a lens so that an image is sharp, or not, depending on requirements.

Foley Sound effects recorded in a studio. Usually sounds made by people in the movie, such as footsteps.

FPS (frames per second) The number of images captured every second on film or video. The standard for film is 24 fps, PAL video is 25 fps, and NTSC is 30 (29.97) fps.

Gaffer tape Sticky black cloth tape, similar to duct tape—indispensable on a film set. Camera tape is similar, but thinner and white, so it can be written on.

Guerrilla filmmaking Usually refers to making films without getting authorized permission to use locations.

HDV (high definition video) The latest video format that gives extremely high-resolution images in a 16:9 (widescreen) format.

ILM (Industrial Light and Magic) Huge special effects company run by George Lucas.

Jib See crane.

Kelvin A measuring system used for color temperature.

Keyframes A frame used to show the extreme part of a movement in animation.

LCD screen Liquid crystal diodes that light up to produce a color image. They are very thin, making them ideal for use as screens on digital cameras.

Lip-sync Synchronizing sound recording of dialogue with the mouth movements of the actors.

Location An existing set that has not been created in a studio. Can be interior or exterior. Favored by lo-no budget filmmakers.

Medium (plural: media) Material onto which your movie will be shot or stored; film, videotape, DVD.

Microphone A device for converting sound to electrical impulses that can be recorded onto a suitable medium.

MiniDV A digital tape format used in consumer and professional digital video cameras.

Monitor Television or computer screen. A field monitor is a small, high-resolution, color-corrected screen for checking lighting and exposure on location.

Monopod An easily-transported, single-legged camera support. Not entirely suitable for movies.

NLE (non-linear editing) Editing system that lets you insert footage anywhere in the edit without having to remove what was there before. Applies to digital and film editing.

NTSC (National Television Standards Council) The television and video format used in America and Japan that runs 525 lines at 29.97 or 30 fps. Sometimes called No Two Similar Colors because of its dubious reproduction quality.

Optical zoom The range of a lens as defined by the minimum and maximum focal lengths. See zoom.

Outtakes Takes that are discarded, usually because the actor(s) made a mistake, but also for technical reasons such as the mic in shot.

PAL (Phase Alternation Line) Television and video system used in Europe and other countries that don't use NTSC. Runs 625 lines and 25 fps.

Pan Following action that moves across the scene, with the camera fixed on a tripod.

Photoflood Artificial light designed for use with film and video.

Polaroids Instant photos made from film produced by the Polaroid Corporation. Killed off by digital cameras, although still used by professional film-based stills photographers for test shots.

Poser A 3D software for creating character animation. DAZ|Studio is a similar program.

POV shots Point of view—showing on camera/screen what the actor is seeing.

Props Items used by actors in a film.

Reflector A shiny surface used to reflect light onto an actor or location as a boost to the existing light, usually to remove excessive shadow areas.

Rough cut The first edit of the film, also called assembly, as it puts all the elements roughly in the right order.

Rushes An ungraded print from a film negative, so the director and DoP can check the footage they shot. Can also be on videotape.

Script/screenplay The blueprint for a movie, with scene descriptions and dialogue.

Shot list List of shots to be completed for the film, usually broken down into a daily schedule.

Slapstick Physical comedy with a lack of subtlety.

Soundtrack Audio part of a movie containing dialogue, sound effects, and music. Often refers to just the music.

Sprocket Evenly-spaced holes in the side of film to allow a gearing mechanism to pass the film evenly and consistently through the camera and projector.

Static shot Scene filmed with the camera in a fixed position on a tripod or other type of support.

Stock See medium.

Storyboard Visual representation of the script, using drawings to show key moments of action in a scene.

Synching Synchronizing, usually pictures and sound.

Telecine Transferring film to videotape for editing. Abbreviated as TK.

Telephoto lens Lens with a long focal length that brings everything nearer (like a telescope).

Tilt Following action vertically with the camera mounted on a tripod.

Timecode Numbering system for measuring frames to help with editing. Shown as HH:MM:SS:FF (hours:minutes:seconds:frames).

Titles Creative way to show the name of the film. Sometimes includes credits if major talent is involved.

Track/tracking A smooth camera movement with the camera mounted on a dolly. Often used on rough surfaces.

Trailer Short preview of a film showing the best parts to entice an audience. A van where actors go to rest between takes.

Tripod Three-legged camera support with a pan and tilt head for smooth and stable shots. Known as "legs."

Tungsten A traditional incandescent light that has its filament made from tungsten, which has a low color temperature that will appear orange with daylight film or white balance. A type of film balanced for this light so the image appears normal.

Video Relating to the visual element of television. Short for videotape. The electronic capturing of images onto videotape.

Voiceover Recorded dialogue that is added to a film after it has been shot.

White balance The control on video cameras that is adjusted to match the light's color temperature.

Wide-angle lens A lens with a large field of view. Particular useful for interiors and other confined spaces.

Widescreen A screen ratio where the width is significantly greater than the height. The ratio of 16:9 has been adopted for high definition televisions. Cinema formats are even wider.

Zoom A camera lens of various focal lengths. On movie and video cameras this is usually from wide angle to telephoto. Originally designed so only one lens was needed on the camera, allowing the camera operator to get the exact framing. On movie cameras it was found that changing focal length while shooting gave a sense of movement without having to move the camera.

FURTHER READING

STORYTELLING

Adventures in the Screen Trade, William Goldman (Warner Books (reissue ed.), 1989): Top Hollywood screenwriter's story of working in the system.

The Art of the Matrix, Wachowski Brothers (Newmarket Press (reissue ed.), 2000): Probably the best storyboards ever drawn for a movie.

Hero with a Thousand Faces, Joseph Campbell (Bollingen (reprint ed.), 1972): The book on myths and archetypes. Apparently the inspiration behind *Star Wars.*

On Writing, Stephen King (Pocket, 2002): A master storyteller explaining how he does it. If only it were that easy.

Screenplay, Syd Field (Dell, (revised ed.), 1984): The standard book on writing screenplays.

Story, Robert McKee (Regan Books, 1997): A standard text on story structure.

What Lie Did I Tell? William Goldman (Vintage, 2001): More adventures.

Worlds of Wonder, David Gerrold (Writer's Digest Books, 2001): Great ideas for sci-fi and fantasy stories.

The Writer's Journey, Christopher Vogler (Michael Wiese Productions (2nd ed.), 1998): Campbell's work adapted for use with movies.

PRACTICAL

Behind the Seen, Charles Koppelman (New Riders Press, 2004): A look at Walter Murch's adoption of digital NLE.

The Blink of an Eye, Walter Murch (Silman-James Press (2nd ed.), 2001): Master editor imparts wisdom.

Directing Actors, Judith Weston (Michael Wiese Productions, 1999): How to work with the talent.

Every Frame a Rembrandt, Andrew Laszlo (Focal Press, 2000): A guide to cinematography by a working DoP.

Film Directing Shot by Shot, Steve Katz (Michael Wiese Productions, 1991): Another standard filmmaker's text book.

From Reel to Deal, Dov S-S Simens (Warner Books, 2003): A guide to successful independent filmmaking.

From Word to Image, Marcie Begleiter (Michael Wiese Productions, 2001): Making effective storyboards.

The Guerilla Film Maker's Blueprint, Chris Jones (Continuum International Publishing Group, 2003): Everything you practically need to know about making a film. Hollywood edition also available.

Raindance Producers' Lab Lo-to-no Budget Filmmaking, Elliot Grove (Focal Press, 2004): Aimed at producers but invaluable just the same.

Scene by Scene, Mark Cousins (Laurence King, 2002): Illustrated talks with renowned directors on their most famous scenes.

The Technique of Film Editing, Karl Reisz and Gavin Miller (Focal Press (2nd ed.), 1995): Practical information on cutting a film.

What They Don't Teach You at Film School, Camille Landau and Tiare White (Hyperion, 2000): Lots of practical tips from the real world.

INSPIRING

Gilliam on Gilliam, Ian Christie (Editor) (Faber and Faber, 2000): One of the more imaginative directors and filmmakers.

Make Your Own Damn Movie, Lloyd Kaufmann (L.A. Weekly Books, 2003): He's been around independent filmmaking for a long time. Lots of practical advice too.

Making Movies, Sidney Lumet (Vintage (reprint ed.), 1996): One of the great masters of cinema.

My First Movie, Stephen Lowenstein (editor) (Pantheon, 2001): Established directors talk about their first major movies.

Rebel without a Crew, Robert Rodriguez (Plume Books, 1996): If this doesn't inspire you, nothing will.

Silent Bob Speaks, Kevin Smith (Miramax Books, 2005): He's funny and can make good films.

Spike, Mike, Slackers and Dykes, John Pierson (Faber and Faber Ltd, 1997): The story behind the success of some of the great independent films and their directors.

DVDS TO SEE

Adventures in Shorts: How a low budget film ended up with an Oscar nomination (www.little-terrorist.com).

Anything by Robert Rodriguez. They all feature different 10 Minute Film School lessons.

WEB SITES

Cinema 16: Shorts by internationally renowned directors (www.cinema16.org).

Lost in La Mancha: The making and collapse of Terry Gilliam's Don Quixote film.

Palm Directors Label: The works of commercials and music video directors, including a book.

Requiem for a Dream: Includes an excellent making of documentary.

TECHNOLOGY

www.adobe.com Photoshop, Premiere, After Effects.

www.apple.com Macintosh computers. Final Cut, Soundtrack, iMovie, Shake.

www.avid.com Avid editing systems.

www.canon.com DV cameras.

www.discreet.com Combustion effects and compositing.

www.dvfilm.com "Progressive scan" after you've shot the movie.

www.finaldraft.com Screenwriting software.

www.frameforge.com 3D storyboard software.

www.glidecam.com Camera stabilizers.

www.jvc.com DV and HDV cameras.

www.kodak.com The film source.

www.miller.com.au Fluid head tripods.

www.panasonic.com DV and HD cameras.

www.powerproductions.com Storyboard Quick software.

www.screenplay.com Screenwriting software.

www.sony.com DV, DVCAM, and HDV cameras.

www.steadicam.com Camera stabilizers.

RESOURCES

www.amazefilms.com Short film site.

www.atomfilms.com Short films site.

www.crime-scene-investigator.net Great for making authentic crime stories.

www.filmeducation.org Theory and practice of filmmaking for schools.

www.filmmaking.net Links and resources.

www.filmmaker.com/DUMPS.html Everything you need to avoid when making a film.

www.filmshooting.com Super 8 filmmaking resource.

www.moviesaskew Short film site.

www.raindance.co.uk Courses for the independent filmmaker.

www.screentalk.biz Screenplays to download and study.

www.shootingpeople.org Networking site for filmmakers.

www.withoutabox.com List of film festivals and how to enter.

INDEX

ACKNOWLEDGMENTS

The author would like to thank all the filmmakers, and their casts and crews, who let him photograph their works in progress. He would also like to thank Adobe, Apple Computers, E-Frontier, Power Productions, and Wildform for their support. Finally, he would especially like to thank his editor for her patience in having to endure his aversion to deadlines.

Quarto would like to thank and acknowledge the following for supplying photographs and illustrations reproduced in this book:
(Key: l left, r right, t top, c center, b bottom)
Page 7, Universal / The Kobal Collection; page 8, Melies / The Kobal Collection; page 9l, United Artists / The Kobal Collection; page 9r, Hal Roach / UA / The Kobal Collection; pages 10–11, Ashvin Kumar; page 12, Sony; page 13l, JVC; page 13r, Sony; page 13c, Canon; page 14r, Bolex; page 14l, Pro8mm; page 15, Pro8mm; page 16b, tripods, Miller; page 16r, FlowPod, VariZoom; page 17, Apple; pages 24–25, Ashvin Kumar; pages 34–37, The Elektrik Zoo, Agile Films, Rickshaw Productions; page 38, The Spotlight www.spotlightcd.com; page 46l, FrescoFilm Productions www.frescofilm.com; page 46r, Plan-It Locations www.planitlocations.com; page 47, Director: Stephanie L. Jones, Production Designer: Kenneth A. Larson www.kesigndesign.com; page 52, Lastolite; page 53t, Warner Bros / The Kobal Collection; page 53c, Lions Gate / The Kobal Collection / HAYES, KERRY; page 53b, New Line / The Kobal Collection / SOREL, PETER; page 68, Live Entertainment / The Kobal Collection; page 69, 20th Century Fox / The Kobal Collection; page 73, Tascam; page 74t, r, and br, Sennheiser; page 74, Zoom Palm Studio, Zoom; page 77, A Band Apart /Miramax / The Kobal Collection; page 84r, Digital Film Lab Copenhagen A/S www.digitalfilmlab.com; pages 90, Adobe; page 91b, Adobe; page 91t, Avid; page 92, MGM / The Kobal Collection; page 93tl, Discreet; page 93bl, Adobe; page 93br, Simon Davison; page 97, DigiDesign; page 99, DigiDesign; page 100, Sony; page 100b, Without A Box, Inc. www.withoutabox.com; pages 104–105b, Nokia Corporation 2002. All rights reserved; page 104–105, "Have I Passed?" script and production stills © copyright Tom Wright / Jason Fairley / Katharine Robinson / Steve Robinson; pages 116–117, Giuseppe Cristiano www.iradidio.com; page 119, *La Vie D'un Chien* stills, John Harden; page 131, Raindance Film Festival entry requirements, Raindance; page 132l, View Askew Productions www.moviesaskew.com; page 132r, AtomShockwave Corp. www.atomfilms.com